Atheopaganism

Community members on finding Atheopaganism:

"I was always getting shamed by other Pagans for talking about the deities as archetypes of nature or human qualities. Finding a group of Pagans that, like me, put the emphasis on giving thanks to the Magic of Reality instead of fictional creation myths, actual gods, and the supernatural gave me a much-needed breath of fresh Pagan air!"

"It has been hugely beneficial for me to discover the Atheopagan community. I've always struggled to name my spiritual path. I love the nature reverence of modern Paganism but couldn't subscribe to belief in supernatural entities or magical forces. Atheopaganism gives rational thinkers ways to celebrate our exquisitely beautiful planet and to live ethically."

Atheopaganism

An Earth-Honoring Path Rooted in Science

by

Mark A. Green

Green Dragon Publishing

2019

First Printing: 2019

ISBN 978-0-578-57197-3

Green Dragon Publishing
114 Lark Center Dr.
Santa Rosa, CA 95403

atheopaganism.org

Ordering Information:

Special discounts are available on quantity purchases by corporations, associations, educators, and others. For details, contact the publisher at the above listed address.

U.S. trade bookstores and wholesalers: Please contact Green Dragon Publishing at atheopagan@comcast.net.

Atheopaganism

An Earth-Honoring Path Rooted in Science

Dedication

This, nonbelieving seeker, is for you.

It is for you in your search, in your intellectual integrity, in your joy and your frustration.

You're not alone.

There is a way to marry the spiritual urge and the rational mind.

Let's talk about it.

Special Thanks

This book is possible due to the support of Atheopaganism's Patreon patrons, past and present:

Abby Pagan-Stocking
Amanda Rader
Andrea LeMeuse
Anonymous
Bethany Brittain
Carl Boone
Carrie Sessarego
Catherine Fountain
Deryn Harris
DJ Hamouris and Buffalo Brownson
Eric Steinhart
James Callegary
Jill Fagerstrom
Jonathan Weber
Katie Frooman
Kiki GardenGnome
Kimba Joy Theurich
Melissa Hope
Randy Pacheco
Sara and Evan Robinson
Sarah Phillips
Selene and Rene Vega
Steve Lewis
Tony Schlisser

My very deepest gratitude to you all.

Foreword by John Halstead

A quarter of a century ago, astrophysicist and science popularizer Carl Sagan wrote:

"A religion, old or new, that stressed the magnificence of the Universe as revealed by contemporary science might be able to draw forth reserves of reverence and awe hardly tapped by the conventional faiths. Sooner or later such a religion will emerge."[1]

I believe Atheopaganism is a significant step toward the religion of the future described by Sagan.

***

I belong to two religious communities: Unitarian Universalism and Naturalistic Paganism. Unitarian Universalism is a religious denomination which includes atheists, Pagans, Buddhists, Christians, and others, all committed to a set of values which includes respect for the inherent worth of all people and for the interdependent web of all existence of which we are all a part. Naturalistic Paganism is a loose community of people who draw inspiration from the myths and rituals of ancient pagans and strive to create religious forms which are both intellectually honest and emotionally satisfying to modern people. Both Unitarian Universalism and Naturalistic Paganism are forms of what is called "Religious Naturalism." Religious Naturalists look to the natural world and to

---

1   Carl Sagan, A Pale Blue Dot: A Vision of the Human Future in Space (1994)

themselves for meaning and morality, rather than to some transcendent heaven or supernatural being.

In my experience, naturalistic religions, like Unitarian Universalism and Naturalistic Paganism, often struggle to find the right balance between rationalism and religious ecstasy. Because we are in reaction to the supernaturalistic religions of our time, we sometimes end up throwing out the proverbial baby with the bathwater—the bathwater in this case being superstitious beliefs and empty observances and the baby being transformative religious experience. When we reject the literalism and pietism of theistic religion, we tend to lose a certain energy or enthusiasm[2], and without that energy, we can't seem to sustain a religious movement. This has been true of Unitarian Universalists, who have been limping along since the time of the Transcendentalists, and it is true of much of Naturalistic Paganism as well.

There have been many attempts to create a viable Naturalistic Pagan tradition. These include the Druidic Order of Naturalism, Toteg Tribe, Gaia Group, Panthea, and Ehoah. But none of them has lived up to its potential. Atheopaganism shows signs of being the exception. Atheopaganism is a naturalistic religion, but it avoids many of the pitfalls that other naturalistic religions fall into, and for that reason, I believe, it has the potential to successfully bring together the structure of rational naturalism and the energy of religious enthusiasm.

---

2   Enthusiasm" comes from the Greek, enthousiasmos, meaning the indwelling of a god.

First of all, Atheopaganism is a practice, as much as it is a philosophy. Atheopagans embrace ritual. Number six of the thirteen Atheopagan Principles states, "I enact regular ritual in observance of my religion."

In a 2015 Spectator article about the rise of modern Paganism, atheist Andrew Brown wrote that what separates successful religions "is not demanding doctrine, but demanding practices, rituals and observances which saturate everyday life."[3] I believe this, more than anything else, explains the decline of liberal religion over the past half century. There is a tendency among Religious Naturalists, like other religious liberals, to favor thinking about and talking about religion over the actual doing of religion. What religious practice they do have, tends to be limited and quite reserved. For some Religious Naturalists, the aversion to theistic religious forms is so strong, that they reject all ritual or symbolism. In extreme cases, even the lighting of candles and the singing of songs is eschewed.[4]

But ritual is a useful, and I believe essential, tool for

---

3 Andrew Brown, "Paganism is alive and well – but you won't find it at a Goddess Temple," Spectator, Apr. 14, 2015 [https://www.spectator.co.uk/2015/02/paganism-is-alive-and-well-but-you-wont-find-it-at-a-goddess-temple/]

4 In a 2012 article from the Harvard Humanist Chaplaincy, Greg Epstein documented the critical reaction from other humanists to his idea of consciously creating humanist rituals: "Even the most seemingly innocuous forms of ritualized practice, like starting each meeting of a group with the reading of a poem of significance to a member of the community, came in for heated criticism. Lighting candles to represent the Humanist values of reason, compassion and hope … was declared strictly off-limits. And singing songs celebrating Humanist narratives and principles was, by some, never to be considered. These ideas are, we are told, 'empty', 'senseless', 'a distraction', even 'nauseating'." (Unfortunately, Epstein's article is no longer available online.)

Religious Naturalists. It can help us feel in our hearts and bodies, what we know in our minds in a way that just talking does not. As Mark Green explains on the Atheopaganism blog:

"We do ritual because humans are ritualizing organisms. We have been ritualizing the important moments and meanings of our lives since before we were fully human. Denying this, pretending that we have somehow transcended the manifold natures of our evolved brains to focus only on the 'thinky' parts, is to deny the factual nature of the human experience.

"We are still the creatures who painted the powerful and desirable/huntable creatures of their landscape upon cave walls, who left the prints of their hands in the caves to say, 'I was here.'

"And it is through ritual, even today, that we create memorable moments of power and meaning. That we connect with our deepest selves, and each other."[5]

This embrace of ritual is what distinguishes Atheopaganism from many other naturalistic religions.

Another thing that distinguishes Atheopaganism is its embrace of ecstatic experience. Ecstatic rituals are intended to bring about a shift in our consciousness, from a state of existential disconnection to one of radical interconnectedness. This is accomplished by using ritual techniques like drumming, altered breathing, chanting,

5   Mark Green, "Why Ritual?," Feb. 7, 2017 [https://atheopaganism. wordpress.com/2017/02/07/why-ritual/]

singing, and dancing. These techniques involve rhythmic behaviors that have a scientifically predictable effect on the human brain. Aesthetics like fire, candles, incense, music, and poetry also help shift our consciousness. Atheopagan ritual combines this neurological effect with sacred content like myths and religious imagery.

When a ritual "works," the participants are able to temporarily silence the thinking or "talking" part of their mind and give themselves over wholly to their embodied experience. Some Neo-Pagans call this state "trance." Mark Green refers to it as the "Ritual State." Once this state is achieved, we may experience a deeper sense of connection with our bodies, with the physical Earth, and with our human and other-than-human kin.[6]

But many Religious Naturalists are deeply uncomfortable with ecstatic experience, as it involves a degree of disassociation from the intellective faculties. Atheopagans, however, understand the proper place for ecstatic experience. Again, Mark Green explains:

"I am the product of centuries of European cultural 'bleaching out' of human wildness in favor of manners, rectitude, forbearance, privacy, and shame. Of steady alienation from the body in favor of the mind. ... Underneath all that, though, I am what we all are: an animal.

"Yes, an animal. A thinking one, but an animal nonetheless, who eats and shits and sweats and fucks.

---

6   Some people have described this state as "enstasy," to distinguish it from ecstatic states which involve a disassociation from one's body or a transcendence of the physical world.

"And as I get older, I find I treasure more and more the times when I can experience my animal self. Singing Dancing. Howling at the moon.

"In ritual, there are techniques that make it easier. ...

"There is great joy in living in the animal self for a time, such as dancing around a fire to the beat of drums. It's a challenge, for bleached-out men like me, getting to that animal self and honoring it.

"But I try, and I encourage you to try, too.

"Own your animal. Feel the breath going in, the happy surge of blood sugar as you eat on an empty stomach. Indulge the urge to howl at the moon, to dance about the fire. Find a way to get outside naked, and feel the sun on your skin. Run your hands over your body.

"Feel that you are an animal, here on planet Earth, not only thinking and wondering at the glory of what we can understand, but grunting and snuffling through the underbrush for something delicious and sustaining.

"Both are true. Both are what we are. Celebrate it."[7]

Last but not least, Atheopaganism strives for community. While Atheopagans can practice alone, ideally their will find each other and build communities around their shared values and practices. Religious Naturalists are iconoclasts and rebels, which can make forming community challenging. But the cultivation of community—physical, not virtual, community—is critical, because group rituals offer greater

---

7   Mark Green, "Approaching the Animal Self," Jan. 7, 2018 [https://atheopaganism.wordpress.com/2018/01/07/approaching-the-animal-self/]

potential for achieving ecstatic transformation than do rituals performed alone. This is part of the reason that Religious Naturalists are suspicious of participation in groups ... and it is the very reason we need them. Our fear of group-think often stands in the way of those experiences which have little to do with rationality.

Mark Green has worked tirelessly to foster community among non-theistic Pagans, both online and in real life. He organized gatherings for non-theistic Pagans (both official and unofficial) at Pantheacon, which is the largest annual Pagan conference. He created and moderates an online community of over 1,500 people interested in Atheopaganism. And he organizes in-person and online events to celebrate the solstices, equinoxes, and cross-quarter days. He's even begun an online course in Atheopagan theory and practice, called "Atheopaganism U." And now, he has written this book.

In December 2018, an opinion piece appeared in the New York Times entitled, "The Return of Paganism." The author, Ross Douthat, is a Catholic and a regular conservative voice at the Times. Douthat asks what it would take for paganism[8] to really become a challenge to the Christian hegemony. He concludes ...

"To get a fully revived paganism in contemporary America .... the philosophers of pantheism and civil religion would need to build a religious bridge to the New Agers and neo-pagans, and together they would need to create a more

---

8   Douthat is talking about small-p paganism, which includes, but is broader than "explicit neo-paganism, Wiccan and otherwise."

fully realized cult of the immanent divine, an actual way to worship, not just to appreciate, the pantheistic order they discern."[9]

Whatever I might think of Douthat's politics or his religiosity, I agree with his conclusion. If contemporary Paganism is ever to become a cultural force, we must build a bridge between philosophical naturalism and political progressivism, on the one hand, and that atavistic religious sensibility which is our inheritance as human beings and which finds expression in rituals and celebrations that are an organic response to the natural world. This is what Atheopaganism strives to be.

What Mark Green has accomplished is amazing. He has created a coherent religious system, devoid of theistic language or symbolism, but emotionally compelling—as the many people who call themselves "Atheopagans" can attest. But the true test of Atheopaganism has yet to come. It is the test of all new religious movements: Can they survive without their founder? I don't expect Mark will be going anywhere anytime soon, so the Atheopagan community has time … time to build the communal structures which will help it survive into the future. And this book will be an essential tool in that work.

— John Halstead, Sept. 2019

---

9   Ross Douthat, "The Return of Paganism," New York Times, Dec. 12, 2018 [https://www.nytimes.com/2018/12/12/opinion/christianity-paganism-america.html]

Ritual for Atheists: A Note of Encouragement

This is directed to our friends in the atheist/skeptic community. Thanks for checking out Atheopaganism!

I want you to know that I know: it feels a bit silly to start with.

When you first start doing Atheopagan rituals as an atheist who has never had a religious practice, it feels contrived and hokey and uncomfortable. It can also feel good, but the discomfort often undermines the sense of rightness or meaning rituals can bring.

I know, because I went through it. It's been nearly 30 years now, but I remember only too well how uncomfortable I was when first confronted with standing in a circle holding hands, talking in flowery language to invisible Presences, drumming and dancing…all of it, the whole megillah.

The challenge for atheists who move in the direction of ritual observances is that the atheist/skeptic community lauds the analytical part of the brain, and many atheists are accustomed to living there as much as they can. *And that is the exact part of the brain you want largely to turn off during ritual.*

Now, Atheopaganism makes it somewhat easier for you. As far as we're concerned, there aren't any invisible Presences, and personally, I avoid unnecessarily flowery language: inspirational poetry is one thing; lobbing lofty thees and thous all over the place is just…awkward.

Where I'm going with this, fellow atheists, is to encourage

you to keep going. Being able to relax and surrender into the Ritual State is a learned skill; it gets easier And the rewards are tremendous.

Ritual practice can open a whole new dimension to life that is filled with meaning, kindness, joy, love and emotional healing. It can make us wiser and better people.

So take a deep breath, and begin. Do solitary rituals so you don't have to feel self-conscious. Then work with your family, or a friend.

And try to keep a straight face. It won't be too long before the thought of rolling your eyes never even occurs to you.

PART I: A LONG, STRANGE TRIP
My Journey to and Through Modern Neopaganism

Becoming a Pagan

I was raised as a rational materialist*, in the household of a scientist and a medical professional. I learned curiosity and a thirst for knowledge early on. The Universe was filled with intricate, fascinating, knowable and discoverable things which behaved according to laws. I wasn't so much an "atheist" as a non-theist; the idea that gods might exist was about as germane to modern life, in my thinking, as pursuit of the Philosopher's Stone. It wasn't until middle school that it came to my attention that there were a lot of churches around, and people actually believed in God. The thought was beyond quaint: it was preposterous.

In 1987, at 25, I was invited by a friend to a gathering of his Pagan co-celebrants to mark the autumnal equinox. I went, and was deeply uncomfortable with the standing-in-a-circle-holding-hands, talking-to-invisible-presences stuff, yet I was also intrigued. The color, pageantry and feeling of symbolic enactment of connection to the forces of nature struck a deep chord in me, opened a poetic, glowing, non-linear state in me that was pleasurable—it felt right (and True) to acknowledge connection to the natural forces from which we evolved and through which we are able to eat, breathe and survive. Unlike the other religious practices I'd heard of, which struck me as miserable, cringing traditions sown with guilt and misery in the name of obviously imaginary gods, at least this was rooted in the objective truths of soil, sun, and seasons.

*In the philosophical sense: believing that all of the Universe is made of matter and energy which follow physical laws.

It wasn't long before I became involved, drawn into a broad community, and spent nearly two decades actively participating in Pagan practice. I became deeply passionate about this practice, writing poetry and music to celebrate the Earth and the cycle of the seasons, and writing and leading rituals myself.

Before I go farther, it bears saying that there are literally thousands of flavors of Pagan belief and practice. Because there is no central religious text, modern Paganism is very much a make-it-yourself religion. Practices and traditions vary so widely that the differences between, say, Catholicism and Mormonism pale by comparison. Nonetheless, there are broad characteristics which are shared by a great many modern Pagans (at least, in the English-speaking world) and it is these I discuss here. I am generalizing, and that is inherently inaccurate to some degree. But in my experience, the attitudes, beliefs and behaviors of the Pagan community I describe here are, in the main, generally true.

What made Paganism work for me was that unlike the mainstream religions, it got a lot of things right. It didn't have a demonstrably error-laden "holy book" to which it slavishly adhered, and it wasn't as sour and mean-spirited as the various cults of Yahweh, steeped as they are in blood and sin and guilt and self-righteous humorlessness. Paganism's values celebrate the natural world, revere beauty and pleasure and creativity, suspect authority, and encourage gratitude, celebration, self-parody, humor and enjoyment. I could enthusiastically embrace all of that. For the first time, I found a community where I felt as though I fit in.

Being in the Pagan community is cool. Pagans tend disproportionately to be bright, creative misfits—the kids that were the genius nerds in high school. They may be expert in obscure disciplines, such as unusual genres of art or music, fencing, smithcraft, brewing, classical history or pyrotechnics. Many paint, sew, draw, sculpt, write, play instruments, sing, or drum. Pagans are liberally sown throughout the computer and IT industries, and Pagans in general reflect the libertarian values often seen among programmers. They celebrate diversity and tolerance, probably largely as a result of so many having been outcasts; a downside is that many have poor social skills, particularly in relation to conflict resolution, and their reflexive anti-authoritarianism often combines with this to create "witch wars" of astonishing bitterness. Many are enthusiastic about scientific discovery—so long as they can cherry-pick the discoveries that fire their imagination and ignore those which undermine what they choose to believe.

In no other community have I found people of such human wisdom, kindness, and fierce advocacy for values that resonate with my own. For all the dysfunction and human foibles found in the Pagan community, I am deeply glad I am there. It is, in my experience, where many of the rarest and most beautiful of human jewels are often to be found.

At first, it seemed to me that the parts that were hardest for me to swallow—the credulity in gods and "magic"—could all be taken simply as metaphor. I—and, I learned through conversation, many of my fellows—viewed the myths and rites as symbolic enactments of deeper truths about the nature of the world and our relationship to it.

All that was fine by me. It was tremendously enriching to my life to join with my friends to ritually celebrate the turning of the Earth's seasons at regular points throughout the year, to remind myself of what each time and season means in the natural world and the agricultural cycle, and what it meant to people long ago.

...and Why I Left.

Nonetheless, there are elements of belief central to the cosmologies and practices of most modern Pagans which I have always had problems reconciling with my core value that *The Truth Matters*. It is these conflicts which led me to begin the reassessment which has led to this work.

Pagans are romantics. Taken as a group, they are deeply creative, and they love to imagine. A typical Pagan is an enthusiast of fantasy and science fiction and enjoys stories and participatory let's-pretend contexts which represent idealized worlds, such as *The Lord of the Rings* and the Elizabethan England of Renaissance Faires. Many are past or current enthusiasts of imaginative environments and roleplaying games such as Dungeons and Dragons, World of Warcraft or Second Life. There is particular emphasis in the Pagan worldview on nostalgic, idealized imaginings of the past, and the meme of long-lost or suppressed "ancient wisdom" carries strong currency in Pagan circles, as the represented antiquity of beliefs and practices is viewed as increasing their legitimacy, particularly if these beliefs and practices are said to stem from preliterate or indigenous sources. There is heated ongoing contention within the community regarding whether or not modern Paganism is a reflowering of old traditions which have remained in practice since indeterminate past times, or a modern

creation based on mythological themes; it seems generally recognized that the latter, though almost certainly true (see Hutton, Ronald, *The Triumph of the Moon*), is a disappointment.

Unfortunately, many Pagans' vivid imaginations and the create-it-yourself nature of their religion lead them to have a tremendous weakness for nonsense. While I rode along for a considerable time feeling comfortable that this was a colorful, meaningful but ultimately *metaphorical* practice, I found increasingly that I was surrounded by people for whom this was not a life-enriching process of working with our own psychologies. Rather, they literally *believed*. More often than not, in my experience, many modern Pagans live in a community consensus reality which renders planet Earth itself as a romantic and idealized self-aware and communicative "Mother", and/or believe that behind the deceptive screen of the "mundane world" exist fairies, ghosts, spirits and deities with which humans can interact. Many Pagans' enthusiasm for "ancient" traditions—real or invented—results in a general embrace of credulous systems of thought which can range from belief in astrology and reincarnation to embrace of conspiracy theories and the idea of literal, physically effective magic.

While many Pagans may be delighted and fascinated by what science reveals of the beauty and wonder of the Universe, what I have seen is that often, they cheerfully ignore

Occam's Razor and the scientific method, choosing instead to seize on scientific findings which appear to reinforce their supernatural beliefs. They'd much rather believe in something because it would be really cool if it were true than genuinely enter into thoughtful and informed inquiry about the nature of the Universe and the human species. They resist the idea of coincidence, preferring to see subtle messages, patterns, omens, "destiny" and supernatural causalities in the unfolding of events, and when it comes to scientific matters such as medicine, are so suspicious of authorities and institutions that they are far more likely to endorse and find credibility in "alternative" therapies, however half-baked, than to trust in the science-vetted products of Western medicine. They accept subjective experience—even experience under the influence of mind-altering drugs—as having a verbatim objective reality which is typically communicative in nature: it is Someone trying to Tell Them Something. And they are highly resistant to the idea that there are more reasonable explanations for subjective experiences which fly in the face of what is possible than the supernatural explanations they choose.

Stir in the heavy romanticism and enthusiasm for fantasy that characterizes many of those who are drawn to Paganism, and the result is a community embracing a consensus reality in which it is believed that gods communicate with humans, magical rituals influence the course of events, past lives inform modern events, ghosts and spirits populate an invisible dimension of reality (the "Otherworld"), fairies reside in the wood, the relative positions of the larger Solar System bodies influence human behavior, and so forth.

In other words, the Paganism I have experienced over the past 20 years is very much an outgrowth of the youth counterculture of the 1960s, and it is no surprise that many of the primary leaders of the resurgence in Paganism were in their late teens and early 20s in that era. The Paganism they have created rejects rationality and authority, delights in tales of the supernatural, "ancient knowledge", conspiracy theories and nostalgic longing for lost Good Old Days (generally imagined as Europe prior to the advent of Christianity), and imagines itself as being a movement which is pushing human society towards an idealized utopian future. It falls into the common smugness of subcultures, feeling moral superiority in relation to mainstream religions and "straight people".

It is sensually hedonistic and libertarian, and places extreme emphasis on what it conceives as its rights, with little emphasis on any corresponding responsibilities. It is materialistic despite its expressed environmentalism, delighting in colorful, sensual costuming and expensive altar and ritual furnishings. The irony of hundreds of people driving or flying hundreds of miles to a Pagan festival (the most common kind of community event, typically camping together in a rural setting over several days to share rituals, workshops and socializing) to celebrate the Earth does not appear to strike any of this religion's adherents as odd, but to be fair, Pagans are human: they feel different, and need community, even if they have to travel distances to get it and turn a blind spot to their values in the process. It must be acknowledged that considerable effort is expended at many Pagan festivals to recycle and minimize waste, and many individual Pagans are fierce in their efforts to minimize their ecological footprints.

It is a subculture with many admirable qualities, oriented in many ways around very positive values. But one unfortunate ethic within that subculture is generally to accept without question whatever someone else may say is their belief. It is viewed as the height of rudeness to inquire of someone *why* they believe that subjective "experiences" serve as evidence of the existence of things that violate the laws of physics.

And this phenomenon worsened. Around the year 2000, with the rise of the "devotional polytheist" movement in the community which directly asserted that being a Pagan required Belief in literal gods, those of us who saw the practice as a metaphorical one felt increasingly squeezed.

In the end, that general credulity could not comfortably co-exist with my skeptical, analytical approach to the world. I like to push on my beliefs to see how they stand up to available evidence, but I saw few examples of this in the Pagan crowd around me. It took a few years, but by 2004, following several instances in which I observed inappropriate and unethical actions justified as "the will of the gods," I was done. I left the Pagan community for a period of years. My altar gathered dust, abandoned. I withdrew from many of my friends and stopped attending Pagan events.

It was after only a few months away from participating in the Pagan community, however, despite my relief at no longer having to smile and nod when people earnestly told me things I found completely impossible to believe, that I found that I missed it. I missed the rituals and taking the time to feel attuned to the passage of the seasons. I missed having a spiritual framework of values rooted in an ethic of awe and wonder and gratitude and humility. I missed the community of interesting and colorful people.

Paganism had been doing things for me despite violating my understanding of the truth.

So I began to think in detail about religion. What does a religion do? What set of elements comprises a religion? And why do religions still have such appeal, even when the nearly all of them are rooted in beliefs that any thinking and reasonably educated person knows are highly unlikely to be objectively true?

Most importantly: once I understand what a religion is and does, can I get back what I lost with a science-based implementation of one? Is that possible?

PART II: THE THING ITSELF
What Is a Religion, Anyway?

What is a religion?

This is a question which vexes even religious experts. There is no universally accepted definition of the term "religion", nor of "spirituality".

Unfortunately, this can result in prejudicial conclusions about their definitions based on the nature of the religions dominating the West, including Christianity, Judaism and Islam. Each of these emphasizes the requirement of *Belief* in a scientifically unsupported cosmology involving invisible persons, magical powers, etc.

Yet such *Belief* is not really at the heart of all religions. There are religions which don't care what you believe so long as you carry out the prescribed rituals (ancient Greek and Roman religions, for example, or American Zen Buddhism).

In my opinion, the only truly universally applicable definition of a religion is a functional one. And so I observe that each religious path contains three elements: a *cosmology*, an *ideology*, and a *practice*.

Cosmology is what is believed about the nature of the Universe: that there is a cosmic ware between Good and Evil, for example, and Heaven and Hell as an afterlife. Or that we are on a wheel of reincarnation until our karma is balanced. Or that sacrificing human hearts will make the Sun continue to rise.

Ideology is the value set of the religion. What is considered Sacred, and what profane? What are the principles according to which one should live?

Finally, practice is the somatic manifestation of the religion: the rituals, the prayers, the holy days, the rites of passage, etc.

Note that *Belief* alone does not create a religion. It takes ideology and practice, too.

Understanding this renders many of the arguments of the so-called "New Atheists" to be moot. Daniel Dennett's *Breaking the Spell*, for example, stipulates in its introduction that he defines a religion as involving supernatural belief, and then goes on to spend several hundred pages beating this straw man.

What if, however, we were to create a religion—a cosmology, value set and practice—wherein the cosmology was *the world as understood by generally accepted scientific discovery and analysis?*

It would still be a religion: it would have values and principles and rituals and holy days and so forth. But it wouldn't be subject to Dennett's arguments in the least.

PART III:
IGNORING FACTS IS A
STUBBORN THING
Why does religious credulity persist in the
face of modern knowledge?

Perception and Faith: Why Do People Still Believe in Gods and the Supernatural?

So why do people *want* to believe in the supernatural? Clearly, many of them do.

The answer to this question begins with culture. We are surrounded by a context which accepts as normal that people will subscribe to belief in invisible beings which are highly unlikely to exist and supernatural events contrary to the laws of physics. Our communities are heavily salted with buildings constructed for the express purpose of indulging behaviors relating to these beliefs and communities of people whose primary point of mutual engagement is to engage in these behaviors. Large proportions of our population go regularly to these buildings to engage in rituals reinforcing their beliefs in company with others who share them. Political leaders are expected to subscribe to such unsupported beliefs or, at the least, to claim that they do so. So the "normality" of this behavior encourages people to subscribe to such beliefs and strongly discourages as impolite (at least) or heretical (at worst) any questioning of them.

But the core of humans' propensity to see evidence for gods is the very nature of our process of perception.

A Pattern-Recognizing Animal

Humans are pattern-recognizing beings. Other animals do this to a lesser degree, but humans have evolved a capacity to store tremendous volumes of memories—both of actual sensory experiences and of imagined experiences generated by dreams, reading or hearing stories, or by experiencing artificially created media designed to fool our minds into thinking we're having an experience, such as movies. We use these memories to help us identify objects and situations we encounter, and to inform our decisions about how to act when we encounter a particular object or situation.

I'll go into more on the brain later, but the key point here is that the way we negotiate our world is to take sensory information and make sense out of it by deciding both what it is and what it means (a threat? An opportunity? Beautiful? Edible? Fun? Frightening?)

Meaning is created in the brain through a process first of categorization of sensory input (stimulus) based on previous experience (to determine what the stimulus is likely to be), followed by development of a conclusion about how to behave in relation to the stimulus, based on memory of real *or imagined* events as well as one's interests and world-view. It is important to emphasize that these remembered "experiences" do not have to be real in order to be used by the brain. None of us has ever seen a dragon, but we'd certainly recognize one if we did.

The two-step nature of the process is also an important distinction. While both a devout Muslim and I might agree based on our previous experience that what we are looking at is a pork chop, we would have markedly different behavioral impulses in relation to it.

Critical to this process is the ability to slot sensory input into recognizable patterns. Our brains create systems of criteria for categorizing sensory input: while there are many different kinds of chairs, we have internalized criteria for "chair" which help us to identify one when we see it. Without this capacity, I couldn't figure out that the input to my eyes and nose meant that I was confronted with a pork chop. If I didn't have previous experience of a pork chop, or if I concluded erroneously instead that the object in question was a soldering iron, it would be difficult to make a good decision about what to do in relation to the object. Neurologist Oliver Sacks relates many interesting stories of people with brain injuries or dysfunction which illustrate the importance of these functions in his wonderful book, *The Man Who Mistook His Wife for a Hat.*

We are, in fact, so dependent on our ability to find patterns in sensory input that *we do it erroneously all the time.* Our brains hungrily project patterns onto incoming data, trying to fit what we're perceiving into understood categories so we can figure out what it is and, therefore, what we should do in relation to it. This is most apparent to us when we experience data which actually doesn't have a pattern: we end up seeing animals (or Elvis) in the shapes of clouds, the texture of tree bark, etc.: a process known as *pareidolia.*

Driving on the freeway, we may peer far forward to read a sign, and do so…only to have the letters rearrange into different words when we get closer, because what we "saw" the first time wasn't what was really there, it was just our brains trying mightily to solve the problem of low-resolution data. Most "divination" methods rely on this phenome-non, generating random patterns of information in which "patterns" are then "seen" and interpreted, be they arrangements of celestial bodies, palm lines, animal entrails, or a layout of randomly ordered cards, bones, etc.

The more general propensity of our brains to find patterns when they aren't really there—or to overlook them when they are there if they defy our beliefs—is called *apophenia*. Here's a great example:

In *The Ghost Map*, Steven Johnson's medical history of the 1854 London cholera epidemic, he discusses the persistence of the "miasma theory" of disease transmittal, which is a perfect example of how a brain function (in the case of miasma theory, the visceral, biologically based revulsion response provoked by the brain when the olfactory center detects methane, hydrogen sulfites, or products of decomposition such as cadaverine and putrescine) can combine with the projection of wishful thinking to "see" a pattern which does not exist to reinforce an erroneous belief: in this case, that "bad air" causes disease. By the time of this epidemic, sufficient statistical data was being collected on disease and death that if it had been considered without prejudice, it would have become clear to those reviewing the data that the miasma theory didn't hold up: why, for example, would some people in a house be struck by cholera, and others not? Why would the disease skip houses on a given street, where all were breathing the same air? Yet none of these questions were viewed as pertinent, and as a result, public works projects designed to rid the city of "disease-causing miasma" led to the diversion of millions of gallons of raw sewage into the Thames, which was the drinking water supply for much of London. Thousands died unnecessarily as a consequence.

The "miasma theory" had been a dominant analysis of the causes of epidemic disease in one form or another for more than 2,000 years. In fact, the word *malaria* is Latin for "bad air". Smart and well-intentioned people over that entire time were so convinced by the idea that even by the time of Victoria, when systematic collection of public health data provided the means of understanding that the miasma model didn't work, they were unable to see what was right in front of them. Their desire to understand a problem and their conviction that they already did led them to cherry-pick reasons for believing what they wanted to believe.

In short, the first part of the two-part perception process, pattern recognition and categorization, frequently either chooses to emphasize information which reinforces what is believed, or interprets sensory data to provide us with false experiences which are created by our minds as they grapple to categorize what we sense. The psychological term for this phenomenon is *confirmation bias*: the tendency to see and lend credence to evidence which reinforces what you already believe. *We see patterns which aren't there.*

...And then we decide what they "mean". Which brings me to the second part of the perceptual process: meaning.

Meaning is created based on our past experiences. What we remember and what we have learned serve as reference libraries which help us to make choices about what to do in a given situation.

However, we are nearly incapable of differentiating between memories of actual and imagined experiences. Research shows that identical areas of the brain are activated through access of actual memories and imagination, and further that imagined memories (dreams, movies we've seen, imagined scenes of stories we've heard) can be as strongly believed as are memories of actual events.

Our capacity to categorize memories as "not real" versus "actual" is exceedingly weak, and when combined with the cultural "normality" of believing in such supernatural events and beings and the natural human desire to fit in and belong (more on this below), it is inevitable that for people who have grown up hearing tales of gods and super-natural events, these tales can be every bit as vividly believed as events which actually happened to them. Add in the well-documented phenomenon of confirmation bias, and the result is a human perceptual array which cannot be considered reliable in any way at the single-person, subjective level.

The combination of these inherent flaws in both steps of our perceptual process result in a deep susceptibility to seeing patterns where there are none and ascribing them to imagined causalities which conform both to our desires and to the cultural narratives to which we subscribe, such as those of religion.

In fact, supernaturally credulous religion is dependent on this phenomenon. Its precepts and narratives connect unrelated events through the explanation of deific interces-sion: person prays for a job, person gets a job, *voilà!* God's hand. Believers in supernaturalism "see" support for their beliefs because their confirmation-biased brains are poised to find patterns which support what they want to believe, explaining these "perceptions" to themselves as confirmation that they live in a world in which unrelated events are mysteriously woven into a deliberate and intentional pattern by undetectable forces.

The conversation between those who subscribe to a supernatural worldview and those who do not inevitably leads at some point to the religionist's statement that he "knows" his beliefs are true because he "believes his own experiences". The problem with this is that *we can't really trust our experiences*. Our brains are so subject to projection of patterns where there are none and self-reinforcing wishful thinking that without some kind of verifiability, we shouldn't be loyal to our perceptions. This is the genius of the scientific method: to avoid the unreliability of individual subjective perception through controlled and repeated experimentation.

Challenging though it is to recognize, "I experienced it so I know it's true" simply isn't a valid statement. If that's all you have to base your beliefs on —especially beliefs about things as profoundly important as the nature of the Universe and whether or not we share it with powerful invisible beings—they're probably wrong.

But for those who accept as literal their interpretations of the patterns they think they recognize, believing in the supernatural is made much easier. And that ease is exacerbated by desire for control in a complicated world—a wish for a powerful, parental ally.

Looking Up to Mommy and Daddy

Another characteristic of most mainstream established religions (which has also informed the development of modern Paganism) is a parental metaphor sown liberally throughout liturgy, imagery and practice.

All of the Abrahamic monotheisms (as well as Hinduism and some flavors of Buddhism) approach the world through a child's perspective: *"We are ignorant and powerless, and must engage in behavior we believe will please the Giant Omnipotencies who rule our world to curry their favor, and thus receive the help we need to survive and be happy."* Stripped down, there is little difference between a Muslim prayer and a Pagan prayer at this level. Both frame the relationship between the world and the individual in a manner which embodies the operational survival strategy of a child, adopting a fundamental misunderstanding of the Universe as a top-down system in which larger orders of scale are deterministic of what happens at smaller levels of scale. The same model is advanced by "Creationists", who insist that a Universe so complex cannot have arisen from simple or mechanical means, and must therefore have been engineered by an intelligence.

It's no surprise that this model for the human relationship to the world has taken hold: we spend the long years of our upbringing in exactly such relationships with our parents, and the world is, after all, much larger and more long-lasting than we are. But in actuality, what science tells us about how our Universe and the structures within it evolve and function is quite the opposite from the top-down monarchic paradigm embodied in the "gods as parents" model, or indeed of any predestined cosmic plan model. With the advent of complexity science, it is becoming evident that the emergence of structures in complex dynamic systems is an inherent, mathematically-driven quality of such systems as they ride the fractal edge between spinning out of control into chaos or freezing into stasis. We see this fact in the escalating levels of complexity which emerge at each level of scale: atoms to molecules, molecules to increasing levels of complexity which, under certain circumstances, are now believed possibly to begin to self-catalyze, forming rudimentary life; thence, increasing complexity of such life, cells which embrace individuals of such life as organelles, cell colonies, multi-cellular organisms, tissues, organs, bodily systems, biotic assemblages, ecological webs, families, organizations, communities, societies, states, multi-state confederacies, entire economies. Or, strictly at the large scale, from undifferentiated subatomic particles to molecules, then larger molecules, dust clouds, stars and solar systems, and on up to galactic superclusters and structures at orders of scale we are only now beginning to identify in the microwave background echo of the Big Bang itself.

As physicist Stephen Wolfram demonstrates in his revolutionary 2002 book *A New Kind of Science*, such complex phenomena need not be the product of particularly complicated systems. In fact, quite the opposite is true: extraordinarily complex behaviors can be generated by very simple algorithms. The available evidence is that rather than being products of a romantically magical generative process, we and everything we know are the inevitable outgrowth of rather simple mathematical processes.

The world we actually see isn't top down. It is bottom-up, driven by its very nature to accrete and evolve toward increasing adaptive complexity within the constraints of the laws of physics. What gives rise to what we see in the living world, including ourselves, does not come down from above and requires no intelligence to manage or steer it. It rises from complex interactions in which any one individual of a system may have no, little or profound impact, largely due to factors over which it has no control. Comforting as it may be to think of a one stop personage to whom we can address requests for support, ours is not a parental world.

Finally in relation to the parental paradigm is the ego problem inherent in the model. The very principle that the imaginary Large and Powerful Invisible Beings that god-believers worship would care about such tiny and temporary beings as humans—living our eyeblink existences on a backwater mote of salty mud whirling about a garden-variety star in a not-particularly large galaxy, in a Universe which contains more galaxies than our Milky Way does stars—is arrogant and hard to justify. There is no reason to believe such beings would be any more aware of humans—or concerned for them— than we humans are of the individual bacteria that populate our digestive tracts.

PART IV: SO WHAT?
What's the problem with people believing religious fiction?

So...What's the Problem? Who Cares if People are Kidding Themselves about Gods?

At this point, it's fair to ask why any of this is a problem. The role of religion through time has been far more than simply to answer questions about the nature of the Universe. Religion has also served to instill and reinforce values, to define what constitutes acceptable and moral behavior, to build a sense of connected community and mutual loyalty among its adherents, to inspire creation of works of art, music and architecture, and to reduce fear through communication of the "knowledge" that some part of the believer remains in existence after death.

At a social scale, it has served as an organizing principle for entire societies; in fact, there is a strong push today to reestablish this as the norm, as has happened in Iran and is desired by American dominionist Christians.

From my standpoint, the values of the mainstream religions are simply unacceptable. They are authoritarian, arbitrarily repressive and rule-bound, discourage individuality and encourage the association of pleasure with guilt. If constrained by the pluralistic and secular democratic political framework originally envisioned by the writers of the American Constitution, however— claims by said dominionists notwithstanding—many of religions' social and personal functions can be beneficial. There are exceptions, mostly related to the lack of tolerance for diversity that is sown into the religious texts followed by these religions and emphasized by their most extreme adherents.

But the Pagan community, by and large, is less that way: more libertarian, more pleasure-positive, less obsequious to authority. And they don't have a never-updated book of dusty frowny rules and threats. So long as we go that way, what's wrong with a little delusion?

My answer to this question is twofold: one personal, one societal.

Personally, I just can't overcome my allegiance to *The Truth Matters*. It's as simple as that. However challenging it may be, it is in my nature to try to become as fully aware of the true nature of the world and of humanity as I am capable. Romanticism is an obstacle to this impulse. The world is beautiful, terrible and everything between; indeed, such value judgments don't mean anything in the broad context of the Universe's steady, entropic unfolding, uncaring and incapable of caring about how we feel about any of it. Embracing all of this, and looking for the very real beauty, wonder and joy that the realities of life's experience can offer should be enough, I think, without having to make things up.

At a societal level, I believe that superstition is deeply harmful. Delusions based in wishful thinking and an unwillingness to consider the implications of available evidence have consequences. In London of 1854, to give one of countless examples, thousands died as a result of well-intended wishful thinking on the part of sanitation planners.

What I see happening around me is that deterioration of reason and the return of religious zealotry is leading us into a renewed Dark Age which will be increasingly characterized by the excesses of violence and conflict which are inevitable when ignorance, superstition and self-righteous extremism are high. Pluralistic tolerance, which was on the rise in the world until the 1960s, is plummeting, and it is doing so as ignorant belief in the face of available evidence becomes a primary driver of public policy and social movements throughout the world.

I believe this phenomenon arises as a result of two drivers: growing dissatisfaction with the failure of reason to address the other human needs which have been traditionally met by religion, and the development of mass broadcast media: first radio, then television and now the Internet, which have collectively enabled mass distribution of crackpot ideas at a greater rate than at any previous time, and have changed the primary modality by which people receive information from the written (processed by the linear, rational parts of the brain) to the visual (processed by the emotional, irrational parts of the brain).

I'll address the former driver in the following section. As to the second, the surging return of fundamentalist evangelical religion in the United States has closely paralleled the rise of radio and television. We are now at the point where no differentiation is made through these media between the real and the fictional, and a majority of citizens are unable to distinguish between the two. "News" sources like Fox News and right-wing talk radio spout hate speech and logically inconsistent, evidentially unsupported ideological nonsense which is taken as verbatim truth by their listeners, who are culturally habituated to believing things that make no sense. Supposedly factual media outlets such as the Discovery Channel carry "documentaries" about "ghost hauntings" and supernatural "unsolved mysteries" such as "mummies' curses". It hasn't always been this way: in the United States, at least, far fewer people embraced such supernatural belief fifty years ago, though more reported believing in God.

The power of these media is fundamentally different than that of the print media of past centuries. Words on a page have never had the level of penetration, immediacy and emotional punch that radio and television deliver. Seeing is believing, and now we can see anything that can be imagined, in riveting detail, through the miracle of digital imagery. And belief has consequences; for those who believe that they will be "raptured" at any given moment, for example, the implications of global warming become unimportant.

In this regard, suspension of critical thinking on the part of Pagans simply worsens the problem. This is a time when bright, creative people need to be more realistic, not less. The kinds of people who are willing to strike out into new territory should do so, rather than wandering parallel to the mainstream highway and thinking they're in unexplored realms.

As far as I am concerned, modern Paganism gets half of the equation right: the tolerant, Earth-caring values and appreciation for joy and pleasure in living are unquestionably the kinds of values that will promote less conflict and greater happiness in the world.

But Paganism, like the religions that preceded it, is built

on a foundation of willful denial of what we now know with high degree of confidence to be true about the nature of the Universe. By deriving from religions of the past, it fails in many of the ways these other religions fail: it encourages credulity instead of critical analysis in questions of cosmology, and frames the world for its adherents in ways which promote insularity, self-importance, and the incorporation of the fantastic and irrational into its communities' decision making.

Which sounds as though I'm making an argument against religion generally.

But I'm not.

Let's talk about science for a minute.

PART V: SAVING THE LIZARD AND PETTING THE DOG

How religions serve fundamental human needs that science cannot.

Where Science Fails

Science's modality of cognitive, reasoning evidence-based analysis has racked up so many triumphs of discovery and innovation in the past four hundred years that many of its leaders have come to conclude not only that science has or will eventually lead to all the answers, but that any questions to which it will not eventually find the answers are not worth asking.

In this, these leaders are completely and profoundly wrong. While they are correct that religion can no longer be looked to for credible explanation of the cosmological and phenomenological nature of the Universe, this has been only a relatively small part of religion's human function. Religion continues to perform valuable functions which science cannot possibly fulfill.

Science and critical thinking are the best tools we possess for answering questions about the objective nature of the Universe and, indeed, about our nature as humans—as products of our evolutionary history, our cultures and our times. These are "thinky" questions, and cognition does the best job in attacking them.

But questions about how to live, what to value, and how to be happy aren't "thinky". They're "feely", and this is where science falls flat.

Proponents of the purely rational as an approach to living, in fact, are themselves ignoring current scientific understanding of our very nature. In the next section, I will examine why proselytizing atheists such as Richard Dawkins,

Bill Maher and Stephen Weinberg will never win their argument, so long as they frame it as against religion rather than against *superstition*.

The social and psychological functions of religion meet innate, inherent human needs. We will not move beyond supernatural credulity and its damage until we have something with which to replace it in performing these functions—something that is not focused on the thinking mind.

Protecting the Lizard, Petting the Dog, and Why Richard Dawkins is Barking Up the Wrong Tree

Until now, this work has been based largely in what we can learn about the Universe through scientific analysis and cognitive thought. Now, let me introduce a curveball idea: this exploration isn't going to get where I'm hoping to go using reason alone. If the task at hand is to identify a rational religion which informs and supports a fulfilling life, elements appealing to cognition will only get us partway there.

An Accumulated Animal

In *The Dragons of Eden*, his book on the nature of human intelligence, Carl Sagan begins with the obvious fact that evolution is an additive, rather than a subtractive process. New, successful adaptations are layered atop those which have developed previously. It is only when a new set of adaptations is so successful that previous ones are no longer necessary that previously evolved functions atrophy and disappear. The latest species in an evolutionary lineage is a cumulative accretion of traits which contribute to its ability to survive and reproduce.

We can see this, for example, in the appearance in human embryos of gill slits. They fade with later development, but they are clear evidence that we still have the coding for the breathing apparatus of our aquatic predecessors in our genes. It is only because we later developed the capacity to breathe air that gill structures are not fully expressed in a formed human.

The central point here is that we are not engineered organisms whose systems were designed to integrate smoothly with one another. Our bodies evolved from earlier forms, building on their strengths and adapting their weaknesses up to—and not beyond—the point where we were evolutionarily competitive. We can see dozens of examples of how this is so, such as the injury-prone spines we inherited from our quadrupedal ancestors, now precariously tipped up to balance vertically atop our pelvises, which themselves have extreme difficulty meeting their dual requirements of allowing us to walk and having the capacity for successful childbirth of young with the disproportionately large heads our intelligence has brought us.

Where I'm going with this is that the same characterization is true of our brains, and this may be the most central fact of our existence. Our brains are not fully integrated and self-consistent systems designed in parallel to work in tandem: they are layers of adaptations, one atop another, and these systems have different processing modalities, different priorities, and can, in fact develop deep conflicts with one another. This is the human condition, the nature of our minds, and the reason we have such struggles internally though we succeed so well as a species. The human brain is a *kluge,* as Gary Marcus, director of the NYU Infant Language Learning Center puts it: a clumsy cobbling-together of systems and adaptations which work *well enough*…but not all that well, really, when compared to a computer or how they might have worked if engineered as an integrated whole. Our brains are not vaunted supercomputers, as some like to describe them: they're Rube Goldberg arrangements held together with quite a bit of evolutionary duck tape and bailing wire. Taken as a whole, these accumulated adaptations work well enough to assure species survival, which is as far as evolution goes. Natural selection selects merely for that which provides competitive advantages to individuals of a given species such that they can survive to reproduction age and successfully reproduce. That's it.

Unfortunately, successful completion of that bare-bones functionality doesn't exactly add up to what we would call happiness. We view the story of a 16-year-old boy who manages to impregnate his girlfriend before wrapping his Mustang around a utility pole and dying as a tragedy and a cautionary tale, not a complete and fulfilled life.

And there's the rub: what we're built to do isn't enough to satisfy us. What we need to feel fulfillment requires that we go farther. People are religious because it feeds them in ways that just surviving to breed—or being knowledgeable and rational—does not.

The Triune Brain

In the early 1950s, neuroscientist Paul MacLean introduced a model categorizing three functional complexes of the brain, each composed of several distinct structures. These three complexes are built in layers atop one another from the very core of the brain to its outer regions and developed in subsequent evolutionary phases. MacLean termed his model the *Triune Brain*. Its elements are the Reptilian or "R-Complex", the Limbic System (or Mammalian Brain), and the Neocortex. Over the past 50 years, our growing knowledge about the functioning of the brain has refined and generally reinforced this broad model.

The R-Complex is a set of core brain structures including the brain stem and medulla which remain largely the same as they were in our reptilian ancestors. It has two simple priorities: *survive and reproduce*. When we are in "fight or flight" mode, the R-Complex is running the show. When someone acts in a manner we describe as "being driven by their hormones", it is the R-Complex, which has no comprehension of following rules to sustain relationships, which is in the driver's seat. The R-Complex is opportunistic, paranoid, and simple in its priorities. It does not have morals. The R-Complex is where our fear, our violence, our territoriality, our reflexive responsiveness to social hierarchy, and our impulse to submit to those we perceive as more powerful than ourselves live. As the earliest part of our minds and the part most completely focused on survival, the R-Complex can—and does—assert control of our behavior when it concludes that life is on the line.

The Limbic System developed in early mammals and became increasingly important as they evolved. Mammals' significant departure from their reptile antecedents is in nurturing of their young, and we are thus wired to care about our offspring, to pursue connection and belonging. In the case of humans, the limbic system has had to be more robust and prominent in driving behavior than in most other mammalian species, because our young are helpless and need our care and attention for many years after their birth. This requires us not only to care about them, but to bond in family and social units which are capable of providing the physical and economic security which will enable our young to survive to adulthood.

The Limbic System feels and expresses emotionally: that is its innovative adaptation. Love, sorrow, creativity, longing, joy and compassion arise in the Limbic System. Its motivation is to *seek pleasure and avoid pain,* and it has built-in systems which release chemicals creating pleasure when social connection—most strongly, with mates, prospective mates and offspring—occurs, and pain when it does not. Interestingly, there are other ways to stimulate some of these chemicals as well, particularly in the creative process. This is probably an evolved system reinforcing technological innovation, which has been the primary function in humans which has enabled us to succeed despite being slow, weak, unarmed (or armored) and having rather poor senses.

Thus, the Limbic System pursues its motivation to seek pleasure and avoid pain through the dual strategies of seeking belonging and connection (love) and through self-expression. The overlap between other-directed motivation for connection and self-directed motivation to self-express and "actualize", as Maslow would have it, lies in *play behavior*, pleasurable pastime which can be either solo or in groups. The Limbic System hurts when isolated, rejected or ostracized, and, through the connections it establishes, broadens the definition of "self" for the R-Complex such that the reptilian brain will react every bit as strongly to protect those to whom the Limbic System feels connected as it will to defend the self.

The Limbic System experiences joy when its imperatives—connection, belonging, self-expression and enjoyment—are fulfilled, and grieves when it suffers loss or privation.

Remarkably, the Limbic System also produces our altruistic impulses. It is a nearly unique characteristic of the human species that we often act in ways which benefit others beyond the immediately defined "self circle" of loved ones, even if these actions do not immediately serve the survival needs of ourselves, our families or larger social units. This altruistic impulse seems to reflect a general evolutionary competitive advantage in our having a capacity to get along with others and see that their needs are met as well as our own, and is also part of a feedback loop in which "good acts" enhance a person's self-esteem, which is a pleasurable sensation and may provide competitive advantage through enhanced valuation by others in the surrounding social context. It should be noted that in nearly all cases, this impulse is trumped by self-interest if the two come into conflict.

Significantly, the Limbic System participates in memory formation by integrating emotional states with stored memories of physical perceptions archived by the Neocortex. Thus, the scent of orange blossoms may evoke a memory from childhood and its associated emotional experience. This associative function has the dual effect of enhancing survival by enabling us to learn to anticipate potential pleasure or pain when we encounter the circumstances which have brought them in the past, as well as creating a "meaning-making" function which cross-references a given cognitive experience not only with its associated emotional responses, but also with experiences which evoked similar emotional responses at other times in the past. The drawing of these parallel associations is the core matter not only of psychology, but of art. It is the physical process of metaphor.

The Neocortex is the conscious, rational mind. Its adaptations are *abstraction*, the ability to imagine projected outcomes of possible courses of action in light of previous experience, as well as to accumulate and integrate knowledge and cognitive memory and to process language. The Neocortex evolved latest of our three brains, and it is what makes humans so markedly different from other animal species, with our capacities to conceptualize the abstract and imaginary, our use of complex symbolic systems such as language, and our capacities to accumulate encyclopedic knowledge of facts and procedures as well as to develop, use and train our fellows in the use of tools. The Neocortex is what most people think of when they think of the mind: it is that which *thinks and imagines*.

The Neocortex uses its tremendous powers to *understand*. That is its core purpose, and it applies its ability to develop understanding in two broad forms.

The first is to augment prospects for survival through accumulation of *knowledge*. Knowledge gained through learning and experience enables us to make better strategic choices and enhance our likelihood of surviving a given decision point. Knowing how to recognize different kinds of dangers, how to use tools, how to negotiate perilous situations, and knowledge of the nature of the physical world all contribute to prospects for longer survival.

The second form of understanding as a core motivation of the Neocortex is to create *meaning*, which I define broadly as an internal narrative about the purpose and value of the person's continued life.

Meaning is important for humans because without it, even though we may have the means and capacities available to survive, we may not see any reason to do so. Meaninglessness conflates with despair and is a primary driver of suicidality, a uniquely human phenomenon.

As discussed above, the power of the Neocortex to create meaning combines with the emotional systems of the Limbic System to produce the expressive impulse. This manifests in *creative expression*, which runs the Neocortex' sense of life's meaning and skill with tools and disciplines (words, paint, sound, movement) through the emotionally expressive nonlinear Limbic System to create art, and in play, wherein we seek pleasure through exercise of the Neocortex' ability to imagine, strategize and create.

What is interesting about the Neocortex' two forms of understanding is that they may relate to one another...or they may not. Consider as an example a physicist who is a devout Catholic. This person's deep knowledge about the nature of the physical Universe nonetheless has failed to inform the meaning s/he has developed about life, which is built around the existence of a God which s/he should be completely cognizant is vanishingly unlikely to exist.

Yet I remain convinced that knowledge can inform meaning, that the two can remain harmonious in the context of a rational, rewarding spirituality. More on that later.

When Brains Collide!

The three minds within each of us do not live in partitioned boxes; they are wired together. The interpenetration of the three processing systems of our minds gives rise to emotions which combine their functions: nostalgia, say, or regret, pride, hope, or shame, which are Limbic emotive responses to Neocortical analysis of events (past, present or anticipated). The different parts of our minds, with their different modalities and agendas, are in communication with one another, and their impulses are not infrequently contradictory, as in our endless vacillations between desire for connection and for emotional safety.

For example, accumulating knowledge and skills can lead to enhanced ability to survive. Assuredness based in such capacity not only reduces the R-Complex' fear of destruction in the circumstances where the skill or knowledge apply, but also has the potential to raise one's estimation in the eyes of others, increasing self-esteem (internally generated Limbic pleasure) and enhancing ability to connect socially (externally generated Limbic pleasure). This is only one of many examples of how the three brains can scratch one another's backs.

Alternatively, they can eat one another's lunch—as when, triggered by Neocortical memory associations with past Limbic pain, the R-Complex is triggered in Post Traumatic Stress Disorder, and a simple backfire in the street results in a panicked veteran diving for cover.

The human Triune Brain is an abstract thinker wired into a foundation of emotional and survival motivations: a lizard wrapped in a dog wrapped in a human. The lizard came first, and when the chips are down, the R-Complex seizes the reins to get us out of danger. And these functions didn't just *evolve* sequentially—within us as individuals, they *develop* sequentially. A newborn baby has no cognitive capacity at all—it is driven pretty much entirely by the R-Complex and the Limbic System, which tell it what to do to stay alive. Over time—many years—we develop the ability to relate effects to causes, to use language, to reason, to think. We become adults through the development of our brains, and cannot be children, whose experience is a product of their formation stage, ever again.

The interconnectedness of these systems and their differing approaches and goals lead to misunderstandings between them which can drive our behavior. One characteristic of our Neocortical minds—so ubiquitous we hardly think about it, yet which can lead to real difficulty in our lives— is our limited ability to differentiate between the imagined and the real, or to accurately gauge the real degree of threat when our fear has been provoked.

For example, a person's Neocortex may assess current circumstances in light of a past traumatic experience and inaccurately conclude that s/he is in danger, plunging the R-Complex into a fight-or-flight response although there is no actual threat. Likewise, the Limbic System may flood us with emotion when the Neocortex reports that conditions have arisen similar to those of a past event—as, for example, when "that song", so filled with old associations, comes on the radio. We may say in such circumstances that a person has been "triggered" or "is projecting", and we acknowledge that damaging experiences may render a person insecure and prone to such inappropriate reactions.

Yet we play on this inability to differentiate between the imagined and the real all the time: much of our entertainment is based on it. We read books, go to movies and play video games to have simulated experiences which provoke our Limbic Systems and even our R-Complexes despite the fact that the events on the page or screen are not really happening. The popularity of horror genres plays directly on our inability to make this distinction, parading illusory reasons for terror which trigger the flight-or-flight response of the R-Complex, resolving when the fear is allayed with a palpable and pleasurable wave of relief as epinephrine production returns to normal and this neurotransmitter is catalyzed. While we "know" in our Neocortical minds that the scary monster isn't really coming at us (otherwise, we would flee the theatre in terror), we don't know it in the parts of our brains which don't understand abstraction and can't make fine-grain discernments between apparent perceptions and real ones, so we go for a vivid neurochemical ride while sitting in our seats.

In fact, a strong argument can be made that all human behavior—*everything* we are motivated to do—can be fairly characterized as efforts to feed the appetites of the three brains. Our entertainments and pursuits shock or titillate the R-Complex, stir feeling in the Limbic System and present learning, puzzles to be solved and stimulation to the Neocortex. Even a sad movie is better to the Limbic System than feeling nothing at all. What are our most-resisted states? Physical danger or pain (R-Complex), followed by dull lack of feeling, alienation and loneliness (Limbic System), followed by boredom (Neocortex). Our social punishments have always involved presenting one or more of the brains with its worst nightmare: death, pain, alienation, and confinement without mental or emotional stimulation.

My point with all this is that a rational spirituality will fail unless meeting the needs not just of the rational, Neocortical mind, but of all three systems of our brains. As we will see, the reason religion is so ubiquitous is that it delivers on each of the core motivations of the triune brain, providing a sense of safety, of belonging, of meaning and of self-expression to its participants. The cold comfort of simply "being right" does not—cannot ever—satisfy the appetites of our triune brains.

Religion and the Brain

From the time we are capable of autonomous behavior as toddlers, we begin to perform ritual behavior. In enacting imaginative play, children are literally exercising their developing Neocortexes, learning to imagine and create. They need to play—it builds the abstraction-creating, analytical and language capacities of their Neocortexes, and teaches them social skills which will enable them to meet their Limbic imperative to develop and maintain relationships. The imaginary connection of ritualized behavior to events in the future or occurring elsewhere (frequently referred to as "magical thinking" in the psychiatric literature) is a hallmark of children's behavior, and persists as religious behavior of adults under the established model of religiosity, associating ritual behavior with hoped-for outcomes, and crediting this behavior with such outcomes if they come to pass. There's really little difference between not stepping on a sidewalk crack to avoid "breaking your mother's back" and intoning a prayer for the safety of someone far away—neither does anything in a physical sense, but each helps the performer to hope for a little control over uncontrollable and frightening circumstances (the potential loss of a loved one), thus reassuring the R-Complex.

Ritual behavior is particularly suited for persistence into adulthood, unlike many children's imaginary undertakings, because as the Neocortex comes online, it develops the capacity to correlate its accumulated experience and knowledge to develop *meaning*, which can stimulate pleasure responses in the Limbic System. This combination of belief and feeling frequently occurs through the process of metaphor: "Action A has a poetic/symbolic meaning of B" says the Neocortex and in response, "ahh, B feels good" says the Limbic System. Examples of B in this case can include such concepts as belonging in the Universe, moral goodness or superiority relative to non-believers, or of being loved by a powerful god.

"This cardboard box is a rocket to the Moon" is no longer tenable without a willing decision to pretend to believe it, once the Neocortex has reached a certain level of development, but "this cup of wine *means* the redemptive power of Jesus" is still viable because it makes no literal claim and offers the pleasurable benefit of a good feeling to the Limbic System[1]. Religious rituals, their symbols and activities

---

1   However, "this cup of wine *has been literally turned* into the blood of Jesus" is more problematic; it requires a full and willful suspension of the brain's cognitive faculties. As I observe it, only heavy social conditioning and external conformity pressures (i.e., threat of withholding of the connection sought by the Limbic System) could possibly lead a person to believe such an obvious untruth. It is much more likely that most who claim to believe such

informed by the thinking/knowing of the Neocortex yet rooted in the feeling/connecting of the Limbic System, produce waves of pleasurable feeling of belonging, connection, meaning, rightness, and well-being from the Mammalian Brain…and help to mitigate the Neocortex' frightening catalogue of potentially terrible fates with reassuring messages that we are not alone, that there is a plan in the cosmos that cares about us, that we have hope for help from a supernaturally powerful figure if we need it.

In short, religion serves the R-Complex and Limbic System with so many of their core objectives that it is no surprise that it continues to persist even in many whose level of knowledge about the physical Universe renders religious cosmology plainly false. Religious ritual, observance, and community offer experiences of meaning, of social connection, of self-expression (in singing, for example) and of safety (both in a social group, and in a larger context as Protected by a supernatural being).

Dealing with It: What Religion Offers the Cognitive Mind

Religions offer more to their adherents than the comforts and pleasures described above. They also serve the thinking mind by providing a moral and ethical compass and psychological technologies for negotiating problems in

---

untruths are simply playing along with the conventions expected by their social context (in this case, a religious tradition), rationalizing that the small fiction supports a larger philosophical truth.

life: ways to weather adversity, survive grief, feel connection and relevance, achieve happiness and peace. In our increasingly complex, socially alienated and technological world, it is these qualities that many of us most long for, and science comes up empty in providing them. In fact, a strong argument could be made that the recent decades' stampede away from reason and toward superstition is a reflection of the fact that most people have a far stronger need for these functions than they do for what science offers.

Maslow observed that while physical survival is the primary human motivator, we pursue other values when survival is secured. The challenge before each person is not just survival: it is how to be happy. Science sheds no light on this question. Science and its products are extraordinary in their capacity to help us survive, but they offer little toward meeting these other needs.

We are organisms the nature of which is to make meaning: it is our successful evolutionary adaptation. Our capacity to assess our perceptions is inextricably linked to our sense of what these perceptions mean to our well-being and our wishes for future outcomes. To project likely outcomes of different available strategies for action, we process our sensory input and compare it to stored memories and knowledge, applying meaning as we do so. *That's dangerous. That would be fun. That's beautiful, it looks like the one my mother had. That would be unethical. That would probably kill me.* These are the kinds of conclusions our meaning-making generates and they, in turn, drive our behavior.

Religion offers the thinking mind a way to *deal with It,* where *It* is the navigation of an unpredictable Universe which can be painful and frightening. For the Neocortex, religion can provide answers to the difficult and fundamental existential question that awareness of the world and our nature poses: *what is the point in being alive? Why should I bother with the effort required to strive in a world filled with dangers, with death the unavoidable result?*

Religion is an Evolved Strategy for Fulfillment

My point, in sum, is that there are beneficial functions which historically have been delivered by religion, even long after it ceased to be the central organizing principle of Western societies. Religion is an *evolved strategy* which enables the potentially warring impulses of the different parts of our minds to have their needs met. In fact, this is almost a tautology: if religion didn't perform practical, effective services for its adherents, it likely would have faded long ago.[2]

Exploring a way forward through a new model will require not only dispensing with the superstition and fantasized cosmology of religion, but incorporating those elements of religious tradition which provide these personal and social functions.

We pass through our lives trying to meet the needs of these

---

2   It should be noted that a primary function of religion in the past (and today, elsewhere in the world, as in Iran) has also been to establish the social order and maintain a power structure, typically ensuring continued domination of an elite. I do not propose to recommend means of fulfilling this function in this essay, as I believe that role for religion to be inappropriate and socially damaging. What is addressed here is religion's functional role to the individual in terms of fulfillment.

very different parts of our minds, which are not infrequently in conflict, and usually without being aware we are doing so. When we are successful in this, we are happy: we say our lives are satisfying, fulfilling, meaningful. But functionally, what we mean when we say this is that we have satisfied the imperatives of our three brains. We have made safe the Lizard, petted the Dog, and provided meaning and stimulation to the Thinker.

Religion, therefore, despite positing cosmologies and supernatural processes which are fictitious, is not simply something stupid left over from more ignorant times. Religious practices and traditions build community among their adherents, provide a reassuring sense of moral purpose and meaning, teach values that create ways of knowing how to negotiate morally complex or ambiguous moral situations, and tell reassuring stories of deific support, survival after death and a cosmic design that renders a given life more weight than merely as the accidental outcome of a nearly random combination of history and genetics. They teach practices which clear, reassure and calm the mind such as meditation, prayer, and ritual, equipping adherents with social and psychological resources every bit as useful and powerful as the technological tools science provides in the material realm.

Religion is a uniquely human strategy which serves the function of helping our three brains to fulfill their motivations and even to get along better with one another. That's a pretty large menu of services, and for billions of people—even some very educated ones— religion continues to perform these functions today.

Which brings me to Richard Dawkins.

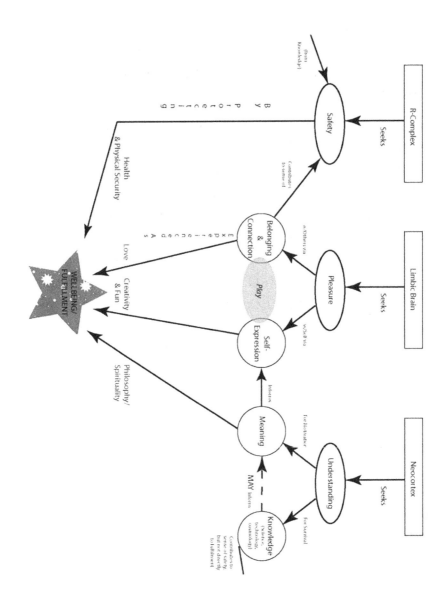

Why Richard Dawkins is Barking Up the Wrong Tree

Before moving on, there are two key points to be touched on here. The first is about the persistence of religion into the modern world, and the second is about the inherent pointlessness of atheist drum-beaters like Richard Dawkins' efforts to make the case against it.

Above, I refer to my theory about the resurgence of religion in modern American life in the wake of the advent of broadcast media and particularly since the 1960s. But there is more to be said on this subject: the primary reason religion has experienced a returned prominence in the world is not just the decline of reason. It is also that reason alone does not provide to the *other* components of our minds the satisfaction it does to the Neocortex. Since the thought-brain is the most recently evolved and least core of our mental systems, to abandon practices which are so comforting to the Limbic System and R-Complex simply won't fly.

The imperative of the R-Complex is to *stay alive.* Traditional religions' teachings cause the Neocortex to communicate a soothing narrative to the R-Complex: *do this, and live forever. Do this, and you will have a Big Friend to bail you out of danger. You will have magical powers*—either directly, through the mediation of the priesthood, or through prayer—*to deal with situations you otherwise have no power in confronting.* To the Limbic System, these religions offer feelings of approval, connection in community and the deeper satisfaction of having the Love of Big Daddy (or Mommy). Religion provides warm, glowing Limbic feelings through ritual practices which evoke feelings of belonging, of meaning in life, of understanding one's place in the scheme of things.

Intellectual satisfaction in being "right" can't possibly hold a candle to such satisfactions for the overwhelming majority of people.

What I observe in many proselytizing atheists is that they are the kinds of people whose histories reveal a strong pattern of pursuing approval (feeling of belonging) by demonstrating intelligence (as have I, to be fair). Many of the most well-known hold advanced degrees and positions at prestigious universities, and clearly get considerable personal satisfaction in being viewed as Very Smart. In other words, they get a positive pleasure-wave from their Limbic Systems when they demonstrate their superior capacity to reason. Where they err is in assuming—as I do not—that others will be wired the same way, and will be wowed by the Big Atheists' dazzling erudition into abandoning beliefs and practices the primary personal functions of which have nothing to do with thought, knowledge or reason, but rather with the imperatives of the R-Complex and Limbic System. That most people do not choose to throw over their religious practices when confronted with the arguments of such proselytizers has nothing to do with ignorance, stubbornness, or failure to be able to reason, as evangelical atheists often seem to imply.

It is clear based on our current understanding of the triune brain that proselytizing atheists can spin logical, evidential cases about how illogical the traditional, credulous religions are until the end of time, and though they may be completely correct in their analysis, they will gain little ground with the public at large because they are not confronting the reasons that people subscribe to religion in the first place. Making the argument as they do, they can never win it: *a prima facie* argumentative case against the existence of god can only, at best, win over the most recently evolved and *least personally compelling* of our three interpenetrated minds.

Trying to talk someone out of being religious because it's not rationally justified is like trying to talk someone into giving up chocolate because it has an unappealing color. Entirely different factors are at play in the decision of the person being exhorted which have nothing to do with the arguments being made, and those are real factors with every bit as much factual, biological legitimacy as any made by the Rational Atheist Camp.

Dawkins and Co. talk as if they believe we are—or can be—purely rational creatures. But we're not.

We're *biologically, inherently* not.

It's not a failing or a matter of choice. Parts of us have needs that bright steely science will not serve. While this does not mean that we should just give up and be superstitious, in my opinion, it means that any real solution to the conundrum of reason and human fulfillment will address our root needs as human organisms and not simply carry on with the nonsensical pretense that we aren't as we demonstrably are.

Part VI: TOWARDS A RATIONALLY BASED RELIGION

Now, based on this understanding of the
nature of religion and the Universe,
what can a scientifically supportable yet
functionally effective religion look like?

Intermission: Toward a Reasoning Religion

So, where have we arrived? We have found that religion does a poor job of describing the objective Universe, but a good one of serving many of our diverse needs as humans—that the values and practices of religious observance support and feed the inherent needs of our brains' interpenetrated systems. From here, what remains is to attempt to define a viable, meaningful religious practice comprising values and practices which support happiness while remaining based in a rational cosmology.

To be clear, this marks the point where I leave what can strongly be argued to be universally and objectively true, and turn to what is more subjectively a matter of taste. Any attempt to create a religion requires core philosophy—what is valued, what is seen as unimportant, what behaviors and perspectives are encouraged—and as such is inherently subjective. The below will necessarily reflect my values. Someone with different values than mine could articulate another rational religion built around different values, so long as they met the demands of the triune brains of those seeking to practice it.

PART VII: ATHEOPAGANISM
An implementation of a science-consistent,
supernatural-free religion

Atheopaganism:
an implementation of rational religion

Extant religions do a poor job of describing the Universe, but a good one of serving many of our diverse needs as humans. Values and practices of religious observance feed the inherent hungers of our brains' interpenetrated systems for meaning, community, and celebration. This book seeks to sketch out a viable, meaningful religious framework comprising values and practices which support happiness, while remaining based in a scientifically valid cosmology free of the supernatural.

A. Cosmology: The Universe as revealed by science.

This is the easy part. For a cosmology, we simply adopt the current scientific understanding of the Universe. This evolves as knowledge is added, but as a rule we do not adopt credulity in any phenomenon without compelling and scientifically verifiable evidence that it actually exists.

Now, I say this is easy, but it contains elements that can be hard for some people. For example, Atheopaganism contains no afterlife. We are *monists*: we understand that consciousness only exists as arising from a living nervous system. When the brain dies, the information pattern it holds (the "self") radiates away as simple heat, and that's it: the person is forever gone.

Atheopaganism looks frankly at death, and does not fear or deflect from it. We die: it's a fact that is true for all of us.

Our path is about living as fully, joyfully and with as much service to the good as is possible, and then to have a good death.

There are resources on the Atheopaganism website at Atheopaganism.org that you can use to plan your will, advance directives, and other death preparations as a gift to your survivors and to make it more likely your wishes will be followed. Click "Death" in the tag cloud in the sidebar.

B. Values: The Sacred

We can't talk about religion—or define a new one—without addressing the issue of what is to be considered sacred: what that means, and how it informs the values by which the practitioner is expected to live.

While many traditional religions seek to define the sacred as an inherent quality possessed by certain objects, beings, or activities—and, therefore, not by others—at root "sacredness" is an ascribed quality: an opinion. It is applied to whatever is highly valued by the tradition or practice in question, and to those objects, events and practices which evoke internal narratives which communicate the religion's beliefs and values.

So: what, exactly, is sacred to an atheist Pagan: an Atheopagan? At least—to this one?

Only four things, ultimately; to me, these are the Four Pillars:

The World. Meaning generally the Universe, but most

specifically the biosphere: *Life*. Evolved from the mathematical unfolding of the exquisite Universe, the interconnected fabric of Life on Planet Earth is to me the single most sacred of all phenomena. It is these systems which gave rise to all humanity—and thus, to me—and which support our ability to survive. All we eat, all we breathe is this, and it is thus holy.

Beauty. Beauty is that which inspires joy in living and which communicates the inner truth of the creative person. Beauty fills our hearts and provokes our minds, strikes us motionless with the recognition of our good fortune in being alive. Bright and dark, soaring with joy or filled with rage, we know beauty because it sets our Limbic brains to singing. It is not optional, trivial or superfluous. It is to be cultivated, celebrated, revered as the means by which the finite and precious moments of our lives are best measured.

Truth. I believe that what is true is of deep and inherent value. It is the only beacon we have to light our way into the unknown future. And the more significant the topic, the more sacred is the truth about it. It is a deep wrong to lie about matters of deep significance: to deny human-driven climate change, for example, or the genocides of the 20th century from Armenia to Germany to Rwanda. It is a deep wrong to deny what is true when it effects what is sacred. This isn't about "little white lies". It's about the tremendous and humbling power of Truth to bring down despotism and corruption, to right wrongs, to advance liberty, to advance closeness between us.

Love. Living as we do, each of us, trapped inside our skins with the endless ongoing dialogue between our various parts, our various minds, humans are subject to a degree of loneliness suffered by no other creature. Evolved as social creatures, we are nonetheless subject to such fear, such doubt, such storms of self hatred and delusions of inadequacy that many collapse under the weight of it, fall to self-destruction and madness.

But love corrects this. Love lights up the dashboards of our Limbic brains and provides us the courage to reach across the great gulf to the Other. It drives our kindest and best impulses, enables us to forgive what we suffer, spurs us to face down the darkness and carry on, to insist that betterment is possible, that the ugly moment needs not be the end of the story. Love brings hope where it has flagged, sometimes for years. It is the redemptive power each of us bears within us to deliver another from hell and into light.

C. Principles: Guidelines for Living

Principles define ethical and moral guidance rooted in understanding of what is sacred.

Principles tend to be practical and specific, specifying how the adherent of a religious practice should behave in day to day life. The 13 Atheopagan Principles are my take on a code of ethics for atheist Pagans: guidelines for living and touchstone values rooted in the Four Sacred Things of Love, Life, Truth and Beauty. They're not in any particular order, but there happen to be 13 of them, a culturally significant number in the Pagan community—it's the number of lunar cycles per solar year—which is kind of cool.

The 13 ATHEOPAGAN PRINCIPLES

SKEPTICISM: I recognize that the metaphorical is not the literal.

REVERENCE: I honor the Earth which produced and sustains humanity.

GRATITUDE: I am grateful.

HUMILITY: I am humble.

PERSPECTIVE: I laugh a lot…including at myself.

PRAXIS: I enact regular ritual in observance of my religion.

INCLUSIVENESS: I celebrate diversity and am respectful of difference.

LEGACY: I recognize and embrace my responsibility to the young and future generations.

RESPONSIBILITY: I acknowledge that freedom is tempered by responsibility.

PLEASURE POSITIVE: I celebrate pleasure as inherently good, so long as others are not harmed in its pursuit and the Four Pillars (Life, Love, Beauty and Truth) are respected.

CURIOSITY: I understand that knowledge is never complete. There is always more to be learned.

INTEGRITY: I conduct myself with integrity in word and deed.

KINDNESS AND COMPASSION: I practice kindness and compassion with others and myself, recognizing that they and I will not always meet the standards set by these principles.

Here are more detailed descriptions of each Atheopagan Principle:

1. SKEPTICISM and CRITIAL THINKING. I recognize that the metaphorical is not the literal. I acknowledge value in poetic expression of feelings about the experience of living, while not going so far as to confuse a poetic description with a factual definition: *Spring resurrects*, I can say, while understanding clearly that there is no such thing, literally, as resurrection from death. Particularly, I do not cite metaphorical or poetic events as justifications for behavior. Poetic expressions in ritual occur in the context of suspension of disbelief—of "let's pretend"—in order to enable creation and maintenance of the Ritual State (See "Rituals").

The core of this principle is *skepticism and critical thinking*: to use reason and the scientific method to determine what is most likely to be true, rather than simply believing one's perceptions or accepting as literally true what is meant as poetic or metaphorical expression.

This is the most fundamental difference between Atheopaganism and many other forms of Paganism: we do not automatically accept our subjective experiences as having objective reality. We understand that our minds play tricks on us constantly, every day, and that even a very meaningful experience may well have been fully or partially a hallucination.

Does that mean, then, that the meaning derived from such experiences is necessarily invalid? No, it does not—it merely means that we understand *that we created that meaning. It was not inherent in the experience.*

Above, I discussed the foibles of human perception at some length. One of my favorite examples is the experience of driving on a highway, and peering at a far-distant sign. At first, we may see that we can barely read the sign…until, as we get closer, the sign "rearranges itself" to read something else. Our brains, working with little data, have projected an anticipated pattern onto what we see, until more data is available and it can then correct to a more accurate perception.

We do this all the time. We see patterns where there are none (apophenia), and ascribe significance to random events (pareidolia). Doing so unchecked by skepticism can easily cast us into a world where coincidences and random phenomena become Omens and Portents…*Someone* trying to Tell Us Something.

We developed the scientific method and reasoning logic to help us to winnow out the false-positives that our brains can often produce from real data about real phenomena. It is incumbent upon us as Atheopagans to keep asking, *how do I know this? What are alternative explanations, and how likely are they to be valid?*

Metaphor, symbolism, poetry, allegory and artistic expression are wonderful things. We use them in our rituals and they enhance our lives immensely. Knowing where they fit in the scheme of things, we can enjoy these benefits while not getting carried away into unreason and likely separation from understanding objective reality.

2. REVERENCE FOR THE EARTH. The second Atheopagan Principle is to **honor the Earth**. It is one of the Pagan parts of Atheopaganism.

There are plenty of reasons to do so. Planet Earth engendered humanity as a part of its biosphere, and sustains us with the food we eat, the water we drink, and the air we breathe. It inspires us with beauty sometimes so staggering that it takes our breath away, brings us to tears. Without it we are nothing, and each of us is destined to be folded back into Earth's evolving story, raw materials for creation of yet more life, yet more iterations of evolution. Even for those few who go to space—perhaps especially for them—the Earth is the alpha and omega of our existence, the only home we know, the wellspring of all we love.

It's not hard to go on like this, and I probably could for many hours. I would describe places like the Grand Canyon and the heights of the Himalayas, Rockies and Himalayas; the wild coasts and high, magical deserts; the jungles and forests, the rivers, the seas, the coral reefs and bays studded with icebergs; the volcanoes and the ongoing marvels of the sky. I would write of the experiences that people have brought back from wilderness, and of the simple joy of stepping outside for a particularly fine sunset.

But you get the point. And love alone is not enough.

The biosphere is currently undergoing a massive extinction event driven—for the first time in its history—not by a random meteoroid impact or the slow seep of volcanic carbon into the atmosphere, but by an organism evolved from the fabric of Earth itself: us. It is called the Anthropocene, and it is a very, very serious matter.

It isn't serious because we may "kill the Earth". We do not have the ability to do that. Though we may (and will) extinguish numerous marvelous and beautiful animals and plants forever, life has rebounded before, and there is nothing that can even put a dent in the population of cyanobacteria, from which higher forms of life would surely evolve.

No, the Anthropocene Extinction is serious because we could very well render Planet Earth uninhabitable for ourselves.

It is for this that we must honor the Earth. We must act in accordance with our understanding that climate change is real, that massive die-offs (especially in the oceans) have devastating consequences for our fellow humans as well as for the creatures we annihilate themselves. We must consider carefully the consequences of having children—especially children who will grow to consume resources at a First World clip. We must resist the endless exhortations of our culture to <u>BUY, BUY, BUY,</u> and rather make do with less, find our fulfillment in culture and community instead of in the accumulation of things.

We must do these things not simply because loving the Earth is so easy, but also because our survival may depend on it. Certainly the survival of as many people as are on the planet now depends on it.

The love is easy. The concern is easy. But acting in accordance with that love can be hard. The Atheopagan second Principle tells us to take up that challenge: to live lives with light footprints and in civic responsibility to the Earth, our Earth, our only home.

3. GRATITUDE. Principle 3 of Atheopaganism is, *I am grateful.* But constraints of language make even this seemingly simple concept obscure and confusing. Grateful for what? When? All the time? How is that possible?

This is because "grateful" is an adjective, and as such appears to describe a *quality* to characterize a person: Bob is red-haired, blue-eyed, right-handed, and grateful. Right?

The way the English language addresses gratitude implies that it is something you either are or aren't, like being tone deaf or French or coffee-colored. But that isn't correct.

Gratitude is something you *do*. If it weren't bad English, Principle 3 would be, "I DO gratitude".

Gratitude is a way of filtering and interpreting information about the world, about our lives, and about humanity in general. It is a learned skill, and tacks sharply against the predominant themes we are presented in our day-to-day living: news channels that tell us all the awful things going on, advertising that tells us how inadequate our lives are because we don't own This Product, stark inequalities in our society which breed envy and resentment, the very real threats to the planet itself.

Some of those things are real grounds for negative feelings. I'm not suggesting they are not.

But a deliberate ongoing effort to notice the many reasons we all have for gratitude is a core path to a happier life. It is a way to keep in context those things we are unhappy about, by filling in all the reasons we *do* have to be happy: a playing child we may see on our way to work, a pretty garden, a sunset, an unexpected call from a friend. A home, food, friends, love. Air to breathe. The flavor of wine, chocolate, coffee, a strawberry. The scent of roses and jasmine.

These things are sewn liberally into our lives, and too often we simply pass them by with little acknowledgement. We allow our lives to be drained of color and kindness by ignoring them when they appear.

There is solid scientific evidence of the benefits of regular gratitude practice, which should come as no surprise. If paying attention to those events and interactions in life that bring pleasure, we become more happy. And when we are happy, we are easier to get along with, more likely to feel motivation to act rather than dispirited apathy, and we enjoy our lives more.

It's not rocket science. But it's also not at all easy if you're not in the habit.

As I said, gratitude is a learned skill, and in our cynical society, it's hard work to develop the habit of gratitude. Like a muscle, it must be exercised. Gratitude is a *practice*. Many examples of gratitude practices can be found online.

Some people have a "gratitude jar", into which they place a note every day listing the things they are grateful for. At year's end, they read them—perhaps burn them in the Yule fire with wishes for more such pleasures in the coming year—and then start over.

Others have a nightly gratitude practice, speaking the things they were grateful for that day either to themselves or with a partner.

But the most important element of gratitude is its contribution to our internal dialogue. When the habit of gratitude is ingrained, the mind stops feeling hokey or uncomfortable about gratitude, and instead keeps drifting back to the reasons we have to be happy, rather than the reasons we have to be angry or resentful or depressed.

The third Atheopagan Principle is gratitude because *it is good for us.* It is good for ourselves, our relationships, our society and our world.

If you don't feel you experience enough gratitude now, there may not be any more important element of self-work you can tackle. Start today.

4. HUMILITY. Principle 4 of Atheopaganism is, *I am humble.*

Humility is a problematic concept in the West, where self-esteem is often conflated with egotism. Being aware of one's positive qualities and abilities is every bit as important as being aware of one's failings and frailties. The Atheopagan Fourth Principle does *not* mean that we should all be excessively critical of ourselves or refuse all recognition for our accomplishments and qualities.

Rather, the Fourth Principle encourages us to *understand ourselves in context.* And there are primarily two ways to do so.

The first is in the context of humanity. Yes, we may be rock stars in particular disciplines or skills. We may even be among the best in the world at a certain thing. But even so: we're *just people.* We're making our way through life as best we can, each of us with struggles and challenges, each of us with unique qualities and gifts. We aren't inherently better than any other person. In the context of humanity, whatever social standing might tell us, we really are all equal. The Fourth Principle urges us to keep this in mind.

The second context that reminds us to be humble is no less than the Universe itself. We are *incomprehensibly small and temporary* when considered in light of the scale in time and space of our Cosmos. When we look up at the stars, we see vast gulfs of space so large and old that our minds genuinely cannot encompass their enormity. We have these tiny lives for a tiny moment, and then we are gone.

The Fourth Principle urges us to maintain perspective, and not to get too carried away either with despair or with pride: not to take ourselves, our travails, our triumphs too seriously. By maintaining humility, we are better able to keep a level head, navigate the hard parts of life without exaggerating them, and enjoy the good parts without viewing them as in competition or by comparison with others.

The Fourth Principle is closely tied to the Third. Knowing how small we really are, and that at root we are as ordinary as any human, the gifts and accomplishments that come to us become the means to tremendous gratitude. How wonderful, that beings as humble as we are granted such opportunities for joy!

5. PERSPECTIVE. "I laugh a lot…including at myself."

So reads the Fifth Atheopagan Principle, and I think it is one of the most important of them.

For, wonderful as it is, hard as it can be, one thing can be said unequivocally about this world: it is filled with absurdity. And that warrants many a good laugh.

Laughter is a tonic so powerful that it gives us strength to carry on despite long odds and many disappointments. It cements good feeling among friends, and eases tensions among enemies. It is simply a good, pleasurable thing. Only when it is meant as cruelty is it wrong.

And it's good for us.

As to the latter part of the Principle, if we can't find humor in our foibles, idiosyncrasies and circumstances, we are succumbing to what the Discordians term Greyface. At that very moment, we begin to take ourselves too seriously. We start being excessively concerned with how we look to others. We lose our core selves to a facade we think we are cultivating.

A good belly laugh at our own humanness is a fine thing. It helps us to stay humble, livens up life considerably, tends to promote optimism. And it feels great.

If there is any major failing the major monotheisms have fallen into, it is their inability to laugh at themselves. Instead of viewing humor as a healthy perspective-balancing release of tension, they see heresy and blasphemy and all manner of scary monsters.

Which I, frankly, wish they would put a sock in, because it's not helping our world any.

Pagans are generally pretty good about making fun of themselves and not taking themselves too seriously, though there are certainly exceptions. I would insert a Pagan joke here, but I'm afraid all of them that I know are blue.

I have less experience of the atheist/skeptic community, but they seem perhaps a little more tightly wound. A lot of the humor I see in their venues online mocks others' religions, sometimes wittily, and others rudely.

As an Atheopagan, I make it my business to look for the humor even in difficult situations, and to seize the opportunity when a good laugh comes along. That's why there are some funny songs in the Hymnal. It's why there are sometimes funny elements in my rituals.

I say, embrace the laugh—lighten up, and look for joy over anger or sorrow when and where you find them. There is plenty of time for seriousness in the world; if levity is overlooked, life is less richly lived.

Laughter brings us together. It keeps us grounded. And it tells us that somehow, things are going to be all right.

6. PRAXIS. Principle 6 states, "I enact regular ritual in observance of my religion."

While cosmology and values embraced are certainly important, the 6th Principle reminds us that religion is something one *DOES*. To be religious is to carry out religious activities: to contemplate lessons, to celebrate the beauty of the Cosmos, to ceremonially observe holy days and life passages, to create art and other works reflective of an Atheopagan worldview.

Principle 6 reminds us that Atheopaganism isn't just something done online, or in thinking about its theory and meanings. We must physically, with our bodies and our time, do those things that feel meaningful in a ceremonial sense: to gather in community (if we can and so choose) to enact the rituals of gratitude and seasons' turnings, of birth and naming and passage to adulthood, of wedding and healing and death.

Some are more formally ritual-oriented than others. I'm

sure there are Atheopagans for whom a mindful walk in the woods is all the ceremony they need to celebrate a given season. All Principle 6 is saying is, *take that walk*. Take time for mindfulness, to quiet your mind, perhaps using the **Atheopagan Rosary**. Light candles on your Focus, and rearrange it to suit your mood and the time of year. Gather with friends to celebrate the Sabbaths, or to hike under a full moon. Build a fire and dance about it with friends, or tell stories, or sing, or drum. Craft something that has Atheopagan meaning for you. Devise clever ways to celebrate that embody the wonders of this marvelous Universe.

Principle 6 tells us, *live the Atheopagan life*. It's not just about ideas or beliefs. It's about doing what we can to make our lives full and warm and meaningful and connected.

Go do it!

7. Principle 7 is INCLUSION. It reads, **"I celebrate diversity and am respectful of difference."**

Sounds simple, right? Don't be a bigot, and you're good.

Not so fast, friend.

From the time we are newborns, we learn to differentiate Our People from the Others. At first, it's because they don't sound the same, don't smell the same…and then when our eyes begin to focus, it's because Others don't look the same as our parents and any other close family members who have been brought into the belonging circle in holding and caring for us.

The problem of the Other is an inherent human condition. It springs from a deep and primitive place in our brains, and leads us to experience suspicion—which, if encouraged, can be inflamed to outright hostility—towards those who seem to be Not Like Us.

Just telling ourselves that this doesn't apply to us is not the work of Principle 7. Our work is to truly come to grips with the complex feelings we may confront in relation to people we view as different, and to deliberately, conscientiously respond to them with compassion and an adamant affirmation that humans are equal. That no matter the gender, color, sexual disposition, ethnic background or religion of another person, s/he is just as human as are we: just as feeling, just as sensitive, just as entitled to happiness and liberty and respect.

It's not easy, and it's not the work of a single episode. It is the work of a lifetime.

In the past 50 years or so, we have seen a great deal of improvement on the social equality scale. But there is still far to go. While sexual and gender minorities may be the cutting edge of anti-discrimination efforts right now, racism is very much with us. Sexism and religious bigotry are, too.

Tolerance doesn't mean we have to agree with every opinion. Nor does it mean we have to treat all opinions equally; the position of the handful of fossil-fuel industry climate change deniers is not entitled to the same respect as is that of the overwhelming majority of climate scientists. But it does mean we have to respect the *person*, even if we think their position is rubbish or was arrived at by an intellectually faulty process.

As Atheopagans, we're trying to live an *optimized life*: a life filled to as great a degree as we can with kindness, happiness, integrity and devotion to the planet which sustains us. A core assignment in that effort is to batter against the structures of our own fear and suspicion of the Other—to push past the fear to welcome those who are different, to inquire with genuine curiosity about their experiences and viewpoints, and to include them in our lives.

Principle 7 urges us to be proactive in this pursuit. It's not enough to "tolerate" difference. Our task is to *embrace* it.

8. LEGACY. The eighth Atheopagan Principle is, "I recognize and embrace my responsibility to the young and future generations."

We're only here for a short time. In the context of the Universe, we are here for so short a time that you need a microscope to view the lifespan of the entirety of the human species. And so our time is precious—and our responsibility to those who come after us is absolute.

Children are extraordinarily fragile: not only physically, but emotionally. Wounds they receive to their self-esteem and their sense of being loved and lovable can and will haunt them for all of their lives. It is incumbent on Atheopagans to treat children with kindness and affection, and to let them know what we appreciate about them. Not in every instant—no parent can possibly do that—but regularly.

Similarly, we need to be thinking about the kind of world we are leaving to those who will remain when we are gone. Is it to be kinder? Less polluted? More free? We make choices every day which affect those outcomes, whether they are big choices like whether or not to launch an activism campaign, or small ones like deciding against the purchase of a new item and instead buying used.

We have to be the kinds of people we hope will carry the world forward after we die, and that means both taking responsibility for our impacts on the young and the world they will inherit, and embodying to the best of our ability the qualities and values we hope they will embrace. Even those like myself who have chosen not to have children—primarily as a consideration of my impact on the planet—have a responsibility to carry ourselves and interact with children in a manner which supports their development as healthy, self-aware, critically thinking, responsible and happy adults.

9. RESPONSIBILITY. The ninth Atheopagan Principle is *"I acknowledge that freedom is tempered by responsibility."*

It means that we are not merely responsible to ourselves; we have responsibilities to others around us and to our society as a whole, and these form legitimate limits to our liberty. We are not the only humans on Earth, nor are humans the only species. Principle 9 reminds us that we are, to some extent, our brothers' and sisters' keepers.

In my experience, the Pagan community sometimes doesn't do very well with this concept. We love freedom but aren't so big on corresponding responsibility. A strong anarcho-libertarian streak runs through the community, and there is often a vehement reaction when someone senses that s/he is being "told what to do".

Well, sorry, folks. That's life in this big, bad old world. It is not acceptable to zoom up a one-way street in the the wrong direction just because you don't like being told what to do, or to rob someone just because you can, or to cook up a bunch of meth because it can make you some money. We have responsibilities to others which trump the whim that might make us want to do so: not because some Authority is telling us to, but because it is morally right to choose the socially responsible path.

The degree of freedom we experience in much of the world—and I have been to some places where this is not the case, which is entirely a different matter—creates not only opportunity for latitude in action, but reasonable expectation of participating in the civil society that enables this freedom to exist. That can include such small and commonplace activities as voting and paying taxes, but also being politically and socially active to increase the justice, kindness and environmental responsibility of the societies in which we live. In the latter, the Pagan community excels: we have committed and energetic activism on a wide swath of issues in our community, much of which is imbued with a fierce sense of commitment to a better world.

Getting the goodies our societies can offer us—imperfect though they may be, and far from our ideal vision—means we're on the hook for helping others to get them, too. With our rights come responsibilities to think about the consequences of our actions, and to actively contribute to the communities and societies in which we live.

Principle 9 urges us to *think about the consequences for others before acting.* As an Atheopagan, I want to be a positive contributor to my society and my local community. At times, that means that my better judgment will override my impulse to simply do what I want. I consider this a fair trade, and an adult approach to navigating the world.

10. PLEASURE-POSITIVE. The tenth Atheopagan Principle is the first that comes with fine print. It reads, **"I celebrate pleasure as inherently good**...so long as others are not harmed in its pursuit and the Four Pillars (Life, Love, Beauty and Truth) are respected."

This Principle confronts a core dilemma of our nature as complex animals with sometimes-conflicting drives.

Because let's face it: *We are built to seek pleasure.*

That's why it's pleasurable.

Our entire modus for action is erected on an architecture of pleasure and pain, be it physical or emotional. We gravitate towards activities that feel good, that are fun, that give us a sense of well-being or of accomplishment or of being loved, and away from those that hurt or feel demoralizing or useless.

This is a core truth of human existence, and it is both opportunity and pitfall.

It's an opportunity because we can *really, really enjoy life* if we so choose. We can cultivate our lives to maximize happiness, to pay attention to the deliciousness of the many gifts which come to our senses. In doing so, we're able to orchestrate for ourselves the reasons we have for being grateful.

The pitfall is that we can be greedy for pleasure, and that greed can cloud our judgment.

Unlike the mainstream monotheisms, Atheopaganism embraces the typical Pagan approach to pleasure: it's good, so long as no one gets hurt. You don't have to feel guilty about it. As Mary Oliver has it in her famous poem, you do not have to be good; you only have to let the soft animal of your body love what it loves.

However, you *do* have to be responsible. Is it fun to ride wildly in an off-road vehicle, ripping up wildlife habitat and dislodging sediment which will end up in rivers and streams? Well, probably. Is it an acceptable thing to do? Not to my mind. Just because something is fun doesn't mean it is justifiable in the context of the Atheopagan Principles.

Is it enjoyable to eat ice cream? Sure. But should you eat a pint of it at a sitting? Well, not so much. Maybe moderate that a bit.

Are recreational drugs (legal and illegal) necessarily "bad"? In most cases, not really. But if you're abusing them, or driving under the influence, they certainly are.

And nowhere in human experience is this Principle more necessary than in the area of sexual relationships.

As Pagans, Atheopagans don't subscribe to theories that sex is inherently "sinful". There's nothing wrong with it: we're built for it, after all, and if evolution alone had its way, we'd do pretty much nothing else except rearing and providing for children.

But sex under irresponsible circumstances is one of the easiest ways to hurt people, damage families and create long-term harm. Behaving according to agreements, proactively seeking consent, being safe, and maintaining frank and honest communications is essential.

Pursuit of pleasure is our birthright as humans. Embracing and seeking out what fills us with happiness is a good thing. But only if it is not at the expense of others, or of the Earth.

That's not much of a constraint, fortunately. So long as we are responsible and remain aware in our pursuits of what feels good, there are incredible amounts of pleasure to be had in this world. Go out and get some!

…Mindfully.

11. CURIOSITY. The eleventh Atheopagan Principle reads, **"I understand that knowledge is never complete. There is always more to be learned."** It tells us to be *curious* and *open-minded.*

This is a core value for anyone following a scientific cosmology, because science must be open to learning that its previous conclusions were inaccurate or incomplete if it is presented with evidence which compels a change in understanding.

It doesn't mean believing or taking seriously any old suggestion. But it does mean being genuinely open to new possibilities if it appears there is good reason for believing them.

This can be challenging. We like our beliefs—if we didn't, most of us probably would have chosen different ones. It gives people comfort to feel that they have somewhat of a handle on the nature of the Universe and reality, at least insofar as what we directly experience goes.

But we do learn new things. It's been a very long time since anything new was learned that fundamentally changed human understanding of physical reality itself at the human scale, but we're always learning more about the brain and how it functions, and that can tell us a lot, too. And though the Standard Model of Cosmology has thus far passed muster with every challenge we have thrown at it, it is at least theoretically possible that some body of evidence will come along to make us rethink parts of it, at least.

My only point here is that if you're going to be scientific, you can't be about *certainty.* You can be about *near*-certainty, but that's not the same thing. We are *nearly* certain that an aerodynamically neutral object dropped at the surface of the Earth will fall at 9.8 meters per second per second. We have never experienced any deviation from this. However, there is always a possibility—however remote—that some new data will come along that leads us to reconsider this.

This principle applies in relation to people, too. What we don't know about a person will always be more than what we do, because we will never be inside their consciousness. Being curious keeps us engaged with the other person, and we can learn more.

Curiosity is a joyful way to approach the world, because the Cosmos is fascinating! Learning more about how it works and its many extraordinary phenomena is a way to deepen our celebration of living, and remaining curious about our friends and fellow humans a way to deepen our relationships.

12. INTEGRITY. The twelfth Atheopagan Principle reads, **"I conduct myself with integrity in word and deed."**

This one sounds a bit stuffy. It's an absolute statement and seems to imply that Atheopagans should be Boy and Girl Scouts. But I really don't mean it that way.

Integrity is actually the path of least resistance for a lower-stress, higher-happiness life. Even though at times it forces you to stand up for something unpopular—or to acknowledge some way you've messed up—more often than not being true to your word and keeping your promises leads to better relationships and higher self-esteem. So it's strictly a practical call: it's a lot easier to be happy if you don't have guilt over secrets or lies or ways you've violated your own values nagging at you. It's just a better way to live.

It's also a path to higher credibility in your social circles. If you're known for honoring your commitments and telling the truth, others will value your opinion more, and will respect you more and know they can rely on you. That feels good, so it increases happiness.

Now, I'm not saying that blurting out unwelcome truths all the time is the way to go. Sometimes, discretion really is the better course, because it prevents people from being hurt or upset unnecessarily. There *is* such a thing as a "white lie", particularly by omission.

But if considering whether to fudge the truth, ask yourself: *Am I doing this to spare the other person, or to spare **me?*** If the latter, it's generally much better to just stand up, tell the truth and take your lumps.

We're human: very few of us are able to do this 100% of the time (see Principle 13), but it becomes easier with practice and after awhile, it can feel almost good to fess up after a mess up. Better, certainly, than having an ugly secret waiting to go off like a grenade when it comes to light.

Behaving as an honorable, trustworthy person is a major contributor to being a happy person. Sometimes a bit more effort, but definitely worth it.

13. KINDNESS AND COMPASSION. The thirteenth Atheopagan Principle reads, **"I practice kindness and compassion with others and myself,** recognizing that they and I will not always meet the standards set by these principles."

In the end, kindness and compassion—rather than anger, judgment and resentment—are the best means to live a happy life. It is far easier to carry around a nuanced understanding of a conflict that acknowledges the humanity of the person who has offended you, than it is to make that person into The Enemy. It may be harder to get to that complex understanding in the first place, but it certainly feels better once that is done than the cold, threatened feeling of having an Enemy.

Now, am I kind and compassionate all the time? Regrettably, I am not.

But I'm also able to be compassionate with myself when I sometimes "fall off the kindness wagon". Principle 13 tells us that there is always another chance to step back, remember kindness and compassion, and choose a new course, without abusing ourselves.

Being compassionate and kind doesn't mean being a doormat. Sometimes, a person simply has to be confronted, or even dropped from ones life, if her/his presence in it is too toxic. And sometimes we have very good reasons for feeling anger or violation. I am by no means suggesting that these should be ignored.

All I'm saying is that both with ourselves and with others, a spirit of compassionate curiosity and an impulse toward generosity of spirit will get us much further along the road to living happily than will their opposites.

If we *orient ourselves* to compassion, make it a central part of our understanding of ourselves and our approach to life, it is remarkable how much easier things can become, and how much happiness life can start to generate, simply in the course of living.

No one short of the Dalai Lama is going to live the Atheopagan Principles (or his equivalent) perfectly, all the time. Nor should s/he expect herself to do so. We all have bad days, sore spots, and events in our pasts which may encourage overreaction to certain kinds of affronts.

Just cut yourself a break, and do better next time. That is all you can ask of yourself, and all others can reasonably ask of you. Compassion and kindness are habits; they require practice. But as millions of Buddhists will attest, they can become ingrained. They can become who we are, and as they do, the world becomes a more livable and peaceful place.

These principles enable the living of a good, productive, and happy life, and the fostering of healthy relationships. There are more, I'm sure, that I haven't articulated here, and you should certainly consider adding them.

Being a moral person is about how you act, not what you believe. And principles help us to know how to act.

D. Praxis: Observances Around the Year

Religiosity expresses itself primarily in two ways: through ritual enactment and personal expression. In the former category are communal ceremonies, observances, holy days, and traditions; in the latter are individual artistic expressions of the spiritual experience, which can be rituals themselves or development of liturgical poems and music, symbolic artworks, etc.

Ritual enactment in a religion lends itself to establishment of regularly repeated structural forms, both so that participants know what to expect and so meaningful traditions can evolve and be revisited each year. Much of what practitioners think of as "their religion" is not just beliefs, but the schedule of observances (or Sabbaths) at various scales, be they once-per-year observances such as Christmas, Easter, Ramadan, Passover, etc., weekly sabbaths or even five-times-per-day prayers facing Mecca. In addition, special circumstances such as naming ceremonies, initiations into adulthood, weddings, funerals and other life events may also be marked through rituals. A rational religion needs ways of observing special times, just like any other.

The eight holidays of the modern Pagan "wheel of the year" present an annual cycle of

holidays tracing seasonal changes, agricultural cycles, and metaphors of the cycle of life. It's not a bad point to start from, rooted as it is in astronomical fact (the holy days are the solstices and equinoxes, and the midpoints between them) and the reality of seasonal change in parts of the world which have a European climate cycle. And while there is a large body of mythology in the Pagan traditions which ties these seasonal changes to stories about gods, the gods aren't really necessary for the cycle to work. It doesn't require them in order to be meaningful and apropos for anyone living today.

For my calendar, I adapt these 8 observances for the area where I live, which has more of a Mediterranean climate, and to add the elements of modernity that the traditional Pagan cycle of holidays ignores. I kept some Pagan holiday names because I know that new ones for the more prominent holidays won't catch on anyway:

Yule (Winter Solstice; equivalent Christmas or Chanukah). The Festival of Lights, keeping us warm through the Longest Night. Celebrates family, community, and beginning of light's return with the lengthening of days). A time to gather together to survive the cold and dark,, to celebrate and give thanks for what sustains us even in the darkest times. It is the height of Winter.

Riverain (Midpoint between Winter Solstice and Vernal Equinox). The Festival of Rain. Celebrates rain, water, art, poetry, music. A time for service to and preparation for what is hoped for in the future (as, caring for a newborn or sharpening agricultural tools). The beginning of Spring.

High Spring. (Vernal Equinox) The Festival of the Newly Born. Celebrates renewal, childhood, innocence, playfulness, discovery. A time for sowing the crops and garden. Per the name, the height of Spring.

May Day (midpoint between Vernal Equinox & Summer Solstice). The Festival of Love and Maturity. Celebrates passage into adulthood, sexuality, freedom, fertility. The beginning of Summer.

Midsummer (Summer Solstice). The Festival of Attainment. Celebrates the Longest Day, arrival into comfort, leisure, relaxation and enjoyment. The height of summer.

Summer's End (midpoint between Summer Solstice and Autumnal Equinox). The Festival of Work. Celebrates technology and handcraft, science and invention, responsibility, physical work. First of the Harvest Festivals (the Grain Harvest) and the beginning of Autumn.

Harvest (Autumnal Equinox). The Harvest Festival. Celebrates gratitude for the bounty of the Earth, the harvest of what has been worked for, the gifts of the World, enjoyment of the fruits of labors. Second of the Harvest Festivals (the Harvest of Fruits and Vegetables), height of Autumn; beginning of transition into the darker time of year.

Hallows (midpoint between Autumnal Equinox & Winter Solstice). The Feast of Darkness and Endings. Celebrates the wisdom of old age, acknowledges the inevitability of Death, the legacy of ancestors, the memory of those no longer alive. A time of the drawing down of nature into the dark and dormant part of the year, to contemplate the unknown, to acknowledge the darkness in life. It is a time for burial/release/composting of what is ended to make room for what is to come, to call the rains back, and to enjoy the spooky, gothic and atmospheric. It is the final Harvest festival (the Flesh Harvest) and the beginning of Winter.

Additional holidays can be added to this calendar as celebrants see fit. I recommend International Talk Like a Pirate Day (Sept. 19), and Pi Day/Einstein's birthday (March 14).

Note that this wheel of the year is one that works for me, in an area with a Mediterranean climate. If you live in Minnesota or Montana or Massachusetts (or Manchester or Melbourne or Milan or Mombasa or Mumbai), your experience of seasons will be different and you will want to roll your own.

The point is to have a cycle of Sabbaths that *work for you.* You shouldn't have to pretend it is Spring when it won't stop snowing for another six weeks. Adopt and adapt as you see fit, or toss the whole thing and go with another concept. This book must never be viewed as dogma or the "right" way to do atheist paganism—there simply is no such thing...nor are there "experts" whose views are any more important than your own.

E. Praxis: Rites of Passage

Rites of passage are rituals that acknowledge a change in life situation of the subject of the ritual: naming a baby, inducting someone into adulthood, solemnizing a marriage or a divorce, transitioning someone into Elderhood, funeral rituals, etc.

Traditionally, rituals have not only been for holidays or personal practice. They also mark milestones in life, when something major is occurring and the community wants to acknowledge that change. Naming ceremonies, passages into adulthood, weddings, and funerals are all examples of *rites of passage.*

This is a tradition that appears to go back a *long* way. There is a Paleolithic cave in France which preserves the footprints of children dancing in a circle, and it is possible that this evidence, plus the hundreds of hand prints—each of a different person—found on the walls of many of these caves marks the traces of truly ancient passage rites. In such caves, the farthest and most difficult to reach areas sometimes contain art of part-human, part-animal creatures: most likely the "revelation" reached at the end of a ritual ordeal.

Mainstream culture pretty commonly celebrates only three forms of rites of passage: Naming ceremonies for babies ("Christening" or baptism, for Christians), weddings, and funerals. But arrival in adulthood (whether legally or biologically) is one we really should mark, as it helps young adults to know that they have new responsibilities and freedoms, and moving on from adulthood into elderhood is one we should consider, as well.

Atheopagans, too, can implement rites of passage into our practices. All of us are born and die. Most of us, too, get married and/or have children, grow into adulthood, and age. Rituals with our families and community to acknowledge these milestones can lend meaning and richness to the process of our living.

It is the "ageing" part of the arc of life that may be hardest for us to acknowledge. The cult of youth is so pervasive and powerful (in American society, anyway) that few of us acknowledge a point when we have become elders, preferring to persist in self-identification as "youthful", if not exactly *young*.

But there is a value, I think, in acknowledging that we have arrived at a Certain Age. It may be easier for those with uteri to mark a definite point of change at menopause, but for those with testes, too, there are definite physical signs: onset of male-pattern balding, perhaps, or the beginning of accumulation of belly fat.

That said, we are living so much longer lives now than did many of our ancestors that the point of declaring yourself "old" may be deferred for awhile. For myself, I have decided that 60—presuming I get there— will be the age at which I declare myself "old" (though I intend to be a *vigorous* "old"). I'll hold a special birthday party that year with a ritual marking my passage into elderhood.

For those of you planning or officiating at a rite of passage, remember to consider what the meaning of the transition is to the subject: is it arrival in the magnificent Universe, or in the sovereignty of adulthood? Is it the commitment of marriage (be it for some limited period such as "a year and a day" of "handfasting" (a Pagan term for marriage), or until such time as love no longer thrives)? Each rite of passage—even a funeral—is a celebration, even if there is loss sown into it. What are you celebrating, and how can that joy be brought out into the community of your friends and family?

Because Atheopaganism has no priesthood, in the U.S. you may need to acquire a legal ordination before being able to conduct weddings in your state. You can do this for free, online, through the Universal Life Church, the tenets of which are 1. Do only that which is right, and 2. All should be free to worship as they see fit. Perfectly compatible with us!

The Internal Revenue Service recognizes the ULC as a legitimate religious organization and your state CANNOT refuse to allow you to conduct weddings as an ordained minister of the ULC.

Depending on where you live, legal requirements for conducting weddings will vary. You may need to partner up with someone from a legally recognized religious organization in order to conduct this important rite of passage.

Speaking of which, divorces are important life passages, too. I've been to a couple of divorce rituals (including one of my own): they were beautiful and heartbreaking.

In each case, as you frame a rite of passage, be thinking about what the multiple meanings are for that passage. Life is complex, and no phase of it is just one thing. Particularly, be careful about assumptions about what the next phase of the person's life is likely to be about, because frankly, you don't know. Some people undergo gender transitions. Some people have children, others don't. In all cases, a rite of passage should be *affirming*, describing the new phase as a positive step forward (or, in the case of a funeral rite, describing the life of the deceased in positive terms).

Our lives are precious, and a central element of Atheopaganism is about not letting them slip by unnoticed. Mark those important transitions for yourself and your friends! You'll be glad you did.

Naming Ceremony. A *Naming ceremony* is a welcoming ritual for a newly born person. In this ritual the baby is welcomed into the community, assigned the name their parent(s) chose for them, and blessed with symbols of the mighty Cosmos and the Life-giving Earth.

To give you a starting point for creating a naming ceremony, here is an outline of an Atheopagan naming ceremony you can use or adapt as you see fit:

Arrival: Celebrant welcomes guests, grounding, statement of purpose of the ritual, establishment of ritual container.

Qualities: Celebrant invites all guests to call out their wishes for the child. Celebrant follows with: "So be it!"

Celebrant issues a Charge to the parent(s) to hold the child as precious, beloved, worthy.

Parents' state their pledge to love and care for this child to the best of their ability.

Celebrant issues a Charge to the guests: will they support the healthy development of this child as a community, and support both the parent(s) and child with love, wisdom and kindness? (Guests respond "YES!")

Blessing of baby:

Have parent(s) touch baby's palms with 1) a clod of Earth and 2) a meteorite, so that they will always know they are a part of the Earth and the Cosmos (these may be gifted to the parents, to keep on the family Focus)

Whisper baby's name into baby's ear

Celebrant speaks blessing of the child with health, love, wisdom, and good fortune for all of their days.

Presentation of child by name to the community (applause!)

Benediction: Celebrant sends off the guests with good wishes in the name of Life, Beauty, Truth and Love–the four Sacred pillars of Atheopaganism. Invites guests to reception afterwards, where food and drink are served.

At the reception, the guests may, if desired, give gifts to the newly named child; these gifts should be things that can be held by the parents until near or after the child's rite of passage into adulthood. Ritual tools, Tarot decks, etc. make good gifts at this time.

Passage into Adulthood. Modern Western cultures, with a few exceptions such as the Jewish community, do not mark rites of passage into adulthood. This leads to a variety of problems, many of them rooted in people feeling uncertain whether they are ever "really grown up". Participation in gangs, having children at far too young an age, and other life-damaging activities are sometimes the result. We would be well served to begin again to mark the passage of young people into adulthood.

I recommend this ritual be conducted around the time of the subject's reaching the age of 18, which is the first point at which the broader society acknowledges their adulthood. While it may be tempting to do it earlier (say, at 16, when the child becomes legally able to drive), it should be remembered that our brains continue to develop until we are around 25. Later is probably better than sooner.

The ritual should be conducted by a circle of adults who have been selected for their relationship to the subject and their family. If the subject has a preferred gender identity, they may be initiated into adulthood by a circle only of those who share that gender identity, if that is their wish and/or the wish of their community.

Rites of passage into adulthood are generally associated with *ordeals* or *quests*. If the example given isn't workable or desired, some other ritual in the form of a challenge or quest is advised.

In some cultures, these rituals involve instilling the subject with an altered state of consciousness. A wide variety of techniques have been used ranging from ecstatic dancing

and drumming to consumption of hallucinogenic mush-
room tea. You may choose to use such an approach at your
own option and depending on the laws in your area.

Here is the outline of a Passage into Adulthood you can
use or adapt as you see fit:

<u>Preparation:</u>

Ritual bath: in advance of the ritual, the subject should
cleanse themselves, perhaps with special soap provided by
the circle of adults who will conduct the ritual.

Fasting: Unless there are health reasons why they should
not, the subject should fast during the day leading up to
the ritual, drinking only water.

Ritual clothing: New ritual clothing such as robes or a tunic
should be provided prior to the ritual (the subject may
be charged with making these themself, though they may
need help to do so). Alternatively, some communities may
conduct this ritual with the subject skyclad (naked) until
clothed with a cloak or robe at the point marked below
with *.

<u>Arrival:</u> The ritual begins at midnight, and continues until
dawn.

First, the Circle of Adults (who have painted their faces
with white clay) convenes, invoking the container of the
circle and noting that humans have done these rituals since
before we were even fully human. The strength of community
and the power of history are evoked as the circle comes
together. A heartbeat rhythm is begun on a drum; it

continues throughout the ritual (drum may be passed from circle member to circle member as fatigue sets in).

Qualities: In turn, passing a rattle, each member of the Circle of Adults speaks into the circle a characteristic, emotion or value they wish to be included in the nature of the ritual.

Welcome: The subject is then invited to enter the ritual space and stand in the center of the circle. Each member of the Circle of Adults welcomes the subject in turn, by name. Once welcomed, the subject is invited to sit (*and given a robe or cloak if skyclad)

Passing of Wisdom: In turn, passing a rattle, each member of the Circle of Adults tells a wisdom story from their life, charging the subject with the powers and burdens of adulthood: honor, dignity, autonomy, capability, political franchise, responsibility. (a few hours.)

Breaking the fast (1): bread or savory snacks and water or wine are circulated to all, including the subject.

Sacred Lore: The Circle of Adults confers the Four Sacred Things and the 13 Principles to the subject, one at a time, passing a rattle, explaining the importance of each. (a few hours.)

Breaking the fast(2) and conveyance of adulthood: When the sun peeks over the horizon, circulate sweet snacks and water or sweet wine to all. A designated Circle member states: "with this sweet taste, we impart the blessings of adulthood to you. You are one of us: you are an adult." (The heartbeat drumbeat, which has been carried out all night, ceases)

The adult's pledge: New adult makes their declaration to the community: pledging to hold Sacred the Four Sacred Things and to uphold the 13 Principles.

The Lasting Mark: New adult casts a handprint outline on gray canvas "cave wall" with sprayed ochre-water (diluted brick-red tempra paint). The paint may be sprayed by mouth, as is traditional, or with a spray bottle. This canvas is rolled up and saved to be used for adult initiations by the same community going forward. Over time, it accumulates handprints of dozens of young people becoming adults. The first time this "cave wall" is used, the members of the Circle of Adults may wish also to place their handprints on it, to establish the lineage of adults in the community.

Gratitudes: In closing, the Circle thanks subject for joining them as adults. They express gratitude to the Earth, the Sun, the Cosmos, to Life itself. The new adult thanks the Circle.

Benediction: A designated member of the Circle declares the ritual complete, the new day arisen, and the circle of the community expanded. May all go forward in joy and health!

Handfastings and Dissolutions. More has been written, imagined and published on weddings (or "handfastings" in Pagan parlance) than on any of the other rites of passage I am discussing in this series, so I will just touch on a couple of traditional elements that I like and let people design their own handfastings to fit their personal wishes and needs.

Handfasting. Handfasting is an old tradition wherein the hands of those to be wed are bound together with ribbons, symbolizing the bond of their relationship. They then… jump the broom!

Making and jumping the Wedding Broom. A festive wedding broom can be made as a keepsake for those being handfasted: each guest ties a length of colorful ribbon onto the shaft of the handle, with their good wishes for those to be hand-fasted. Later, when the broom is complete, those being handfasted traditionally "jump the broom": it is held about a foot above the ground, and they—with their hands still bound together handfast—leap over it, to the applause of the wedding guests.

A *Year and a Day:* In some Pagan communities, people may choose a "trial marriage" of a year and a day of commitment, to see how well it will work before making a longer-term commitment. Obviously, this isn't a legal marriage.

Dissolution ceremonies are rare in our society, but if those whose marriage is to be dissolved are able and willing, they can provide a sense of closure at the end of a relationship that is no longer working.

Dissolution ceremonies should be 1) short and 2) final. During or before them, rings and family heirlooms should be returned.

Here is an outline for a simple dissolution ceremony for a separating couple. The officiant may have to keep a firm hand on the proceedings if the participants are angry and hurt. The ceremony should include members from the couple's community to support them and witness their dissolution.

Preparation:

A large, inexpensive vase of water is prepared, with two empty glasses. A towel large enough to swath the vase and a large rubber band are at hand.

Arrival:

Officiant: We are gathered here today to achieve the final separation of the marriage of _____ and _____. Friends have joined with us to witness the ending of their time in committed relationship, and to support their moving on to new chapters in their lives.

Qualities:

Officiant solicits spoken emotions, values and characteristics from the participants which they would like to inform the dissolution process.

Working:

A ribbon from the original handfasting is cast into the vase of water (If possible, the couple's rings may be tied into the ribbon to keep it from floating out). Officiant states: this is the relationship you have shared.

Officiant then empties the water from the vase in equal amounts into the two glasses and gives one to each member of the couple, saying, now it is time to take yourselves away from what has gone before.

Officiant swathes the vase—now empty except for the ribbon—in the towel, binds the bundle closed with a rubber band, and puts it into the hands (all four) of the divorcing couple. They raise it above their heads and then cast it to the ground to break the vase, ending their relationship.

The couple drink their water.

Gratitudes: Officiant solicits from each of the divorcing couple an expression of gratitude for what they have learned and experienced with the other.

Benediction: It is complete. Officiant declares the work to be done, sending all participants forth to live full, happy and wise lives.

Passages into Elderhood. The Passage to Elderhood occurs when the subject thereof feels ready to take on that identity. There is no hard and fast rule about an age at which a person is an "elder"; some may never feel that they are.

Personally, I have decided that when I turn 60, it'll be time for mine.

This Rite is one of *acknowledgement*. In it, the achievements and efforts of the person along the way to becoming an Elder are recognized and celebrated. There is no "ordeal" involved; the subject has already lived many ordeals and survived them.

The passage into elderhood should be conducted by a circle of friends and family. The organizers may choose to include only those who have attained adulthood, or also to include younger members of the subject's loved ones.

This ritual should be conducted in a comfortable, convivial environment. Age has privileges! Comfortable seats in a circle about the subject (also comfortably seated, perhaps in a swiveling chair so they can turn to face each speaker) are appropriate. This ritual doesn't have a single "officiant", but rather is a shared activity of all participants.

Arrival (Speaker 1): We are here, atop the accumulation of time. In their life, _____ has seen a, b, c, d, e, f… (list historical, cultural and technological changes). We come to this moment now filled with memories, with history. We arrive in this moment rich with hard-won knowledge. We are here, now, on Planet Earth at this very moment, the Now, to celebrate our kindred who is becoming Elder.

Qualities (Speaker 2): May we be imbued with kindness as we do this. May we be filled with courage and honesty. May we remember what is valuable to remember, and share what we have learned. May Love, and Truth, and Beauty, and the Sacred Cosmos inform our words and deeds.

Working: each segment taken by a different speaker.

We acknowledge your struggle: Speaker 3 invites the new Elder to tell a story involving personal emotional challenge.

We acknowledge your work: Speaker 4 invites the new Elder to tell a story about their career and creative efforts.

We acknowledge your wisdom: Speaker 5 states the ways they have seen the new Elder demonstrate wisdom.

We acknowledge the value you have to contribute going forward: All speakers state the ways they see the new Elder contributing to the world and the community. If gifts are to be given, they are given here.

New Elder speaks on their commitments to contribute going forward, their interests, and their passions.

Gratitude: While passing around food and drink, members of the circle express gratitude for the admirable qualities of the new Elder. When it is their turn, the new Elder expresses gratitude for the things in life that have brought it to the point of Elderhood.

Benediction (Speaker 1): We are grateful to the Cosmos for our lives, to the good Earth and human innovation for the longevity which has led us to reach this point in our lives. In the names of Love, and Life, and Beauty, and Truth, we welcome into the world the Elder _____, our kindred. May we go forth in wisdom and joy!

Memorial and Funeral Services. This rite of passage is structured more like a traditional memorial service because funerals typically have more attendees than can be accommodated in an Atheopagan circle. A smaller and more intimate Atheopagan circle might be conducted around the grave before burial (if the body is to be buried), but this post is focused on the memorial rite.

Of all the life passages described in this series, this is the only one that is guaranteed to all of us: we all die. Some of us do so even before we are born. This rite of passage is meant to comfort the living, to celebrate the dead, and to contextualize living and dying in the great story of Life on Earth.

When planning a memorial or funeral service, there are many considerations: what did the deceased feel were their greatest accomplishments in life? How did their atheist spirituality fit in with the rest of their family? What were their wishes for a memorial, if they left them? If for a stillbirth or miscarriage, what are the messages the parent(s) would like to give to the deceased?

Here is a general outline for an Atheopagan memorial service:

Gathering/Arrival: play music that was loved by the deceased during this period*. It doesn't have to be sad music! A memorial is a celebration of a life.

Welcoming remarks by you, the officiant. Bid everyone welcome and ask them to be seated. Welcome the family in particular, and if there are any "dignitaries" or special friends to the family, welcome them, too. Have everyone take a deep breath, and blow it out: we are here, in this place today, in the presence of the profound reality that is death. In our sorrow, we come together today to celebrate the life of _____.

<u>Poem or prose reading celebrating the magnificence of existence:</u> This is where the "Pagan" part of the ritual comes in. It is a reminder of the beauty of Life on Earth, in this extraordinary Cosmos. That we live here, surrounded by wonders, for a brief time, and then dissolve back into the Cosmos from which we came.

<u>Musical Interlude:</u> A song or instrumental piece–guests may be invited to sing along if the organizers wish it. Be sure to provide music sheets to guests if you choose this option.

<u>Eulogy:</u> A prepared speech to memorialize and celebrate the life of the deceased. Usually delivered by a family member or close friend. May include description of the deceased's Atheopaganism and what it meant to them, and/or any final words the deceased left behind for their community.

<u>Poem or prose reading</u>

Officiant <u>invites</u> guests up to share personal memories

<u>Personal Memories:</u> spontaneous memories shared by guests

<u>Musical Interlude:</u> another song or instrumental piece, possibly with guests singing.

<u>Benediction:</u> (Literally, "saying a good word"): a closing statement by the officiant acknowledging the love and respect that has been expressed for the deceased, gratitude for the deceased's life, with well-wishes for the family and loved ones, an adjuration to embrace our precious lives,

and an invitation to the reception following the memorial (or burial service if that is to follow)

Restart gathering music as attendees stand and prepare to leave.

Praxis: Contemplative Practices

There is great value in meditative/contemplative practice. If religious ritual is intended to create the state of *heightened presence*, practicing mindfulness and being present in the moment is a way to develop the ability to experience greater impact from such rituals.

One such meditative practice is the use of a rosary, or prayer beads, while repeating a contemplative poem. Here are instructions for one such implementation, the Atheopagan Rosary:

I find that—when I can make myself do it—a daily mindfulness meditation adds a great deal to my experience of living, and I'd like to find a way to do that on most days, if not all. So I'm stealing from true masters of ritual technology—the Catholic Church and the Tibetan Buddhists—to create this Atheopagan rosary.

The bead string itself is simple: 3 courses of 13 beads, with the 13th always being recognizable as the last of a series. I like beautiful things, so I went to a bead store and bought pretty beads mostly of fused glass and semi-precious stones; they feel solid and weighty in the hand. A larger one could certainly be made; I like prime numbers, so if I were going to make a bigger rosary I would probably go for 7 courses (91 beads). I place the rosary on my Focus (altar) when it isn't in use.

To "say" the Atheopagan rosary, speak or think one line for each bead. I go through the meditation 3 times (3 repetitions of the 3 courses).

I drew the meditation for this rosary from Buddhist sources cited in a mindfulness class I took, as well as the 13 Principles of Atheopaganism as I practice them. You can write your own, of course, and I use different ones for seasonal sabbaths or other uses. But the main point is the use of repetition to reprogram your brain to embrace the qualities in the meditation: to make a better world for you, for those around you, and for all of us.

NOTE: If you're like me, be ready for a lot of internal chatter disputing these statements—that's why they're powerful. With time, that fades, and you start to experience the meditation's statements as true.

First two courses of 13:

May my heart be happy

May my mind be at ease

May my body be healthy

May I know peace today

May those I touch know kindness

May the Cosmos be honored

May the good Earth be revered

May my heart be grateful

May I act with integrity

May I know that I am loved,

That I deserve love.

That all deserve love.

May all I am and do, be of love.

(repeat)

Last course of 13:

My heart is happy

My mind is at ease

My body is healthy

Peace is with me today

I am kind to those around me

The Cosmos fills me with wonder

The good Earth is generous

My heart is grateful

I act with integrity

I am loved,

I deserve love,

All deserve love.

All I am and do is of love.

Praxis: Rituals

Every religion practices rituals: formalized procedures
the intent of which is to provoke and maintain a Limbic
mental state of liminal presence (which I have termed the
"Ritual state"). Activities in religious rituals take place in a
manner participants come to know and anticipate, fostering
a sense of familiarity with what is happening and what will
come next. This contributes to the sense of safety necessary
before this ritual state may fully be entered.

So—what is the Ritual State? It is characterized by heightened
senses and extreme focus on the present moment, reduced
self-consciousness, heightened recognition of patterns (and
their recognition as meaningful), and strong feelings of
enjoyment, power and ability.

It is, in fact, a brain state which has been studied a great
deal, and is known by psychologists as *flow*: a state of complete
immersion and enjoyment in what one is doing at the
present moment. It is the result of a cascade of good-feeling
and performance-enhancing neurotransmitters such as
serotonin, dopamine and norepinephrine being emitted in
the brain.

We have all experienced flow. It is, in fact, the state humans pursue almost continually; our recreation is full of
efforts to come vividly into the present moment and enjoy
what one is doing.

The Ritual State is flow. The *induction phase* of a ritual
(which I call Arrival—see below) is designed to promote
celebrants' entry into flow through the use of ritual tech-

nologies, after which the work of the ritual can begin.

Creation of a successful ritual is rather like cooking a delicious meal: it can be viewed in some ways as a science, in that it is possible to follow a series of repeatable programmed steps—a recipe—to do it. Below, I will describe a framework which may be followed as one suggestion for how effective ritual may be enacted, and if you use it, it will work.

However, ritual is not *only* a science: it is also an art.

We all know that the best food isn't merely competently assembled—it is created by someone inspired and who has a deep, intuitive understanding of the processes that lead to delicious flavors and textures. Truly transformational and moving ritual, similarly, arises when inspired creators informed by deep understanding of how to work with human psychology work effectively and subtly to transport participants with the meaning, flavor and vivid reality of the experience they share with fellow celebrants.

And that is why this section is not a "cookbook". This work is not intended to provide a script—all the spoken words, songs, movements and other activities—for creation of a ritual on a particular theme.

Rather, what you find here is a treatise meant to communicate key concepts which must be understood in order to be a good ritual "cook": to understand processes and outcomes for successful ritual enactment instead of merely prescribing actions. While cooking can be done successfully merely by adhering to a set of instructions, ritual works best when it is largely improvisational, working from an outline of expected steps and *flowing* effortlessly, carrying its participants along from one phase to another. And one thing that can interrupt that flow is for leaders/facilitators of the ritual to be locked into referring back to written notes in order to know what happens next.

So think of this as a description of fundamental principles and ideas to inform your own creation of rituals. And then start doing them, and learning along the way. It is the only way to become good at it.

Because after all, it is far better to be a skilled cook than merely to have a good recipe book.

1. What is a Ritual?

Rituals are *symbolic acts carried out in an intentional manner to evoke metaphorical or symbolic meaning in the celebrant* or celebrants. Purposes of rituals are often to celebrate a particular season or holiday and its metaphorical meanings, to observe a life passage such as a birth, wedding or death, or simply to offer awe, humility and reverence to the great Cosmos of which we are all a part.

Celebrating ritual enriches a life and helps to bring a sense of meaning to the passage of time. Rituals can reinforce devotion to values and bring renewed confidence in goals and interpersonal commitments.

As with all elements of Atheopaganism, we do this to enrich our lives and because it works: there is solid scientific evidence for the benefits and effectiveness of ritual in a person's life. (see http://www.scientificamerican.com/article/

why-rituals-work/)

The goal of Atheopagan ritual design is to create a state in participants to feel both connected to the inner truth of themselves and the meaning they find in their lives *and to be able unselfconsciously to express this truth with authenticity:* to connect with one another, process transformative understanding such as healing or grief, celebrate gratitude, awe and wonder at the beauty and magnificence of the Universe, and otherwise to live and express, in that moment, the fullness of who they are as individuals.

2. Why Do Rituals?

Well, first of all because it feels good.

Secondly, because it enriches our lives to celebrate around the seasons and ritualize the passages in our lives. It enhances happiness.

But perhaps most importantly, because *it's good for us.* Not only are the community and celebration and connection and expression and openness and love that can be experienced in ritual circle a joy in life, but ritual can also be profoundly healing of psychological wounds, as well as helping to facilitate healing of physical ones. It's powerful. It works.

So my recommendation in terms of making rituals meaningful and healing and transformative is to **GO FOR DEPTH.** Ask people to inhabit their hearts and work with what is there. Don't be afraid to trust the work.

Here's an example; one year at Pantheacon, a convention

comprising the largest indoor gathering of Pagans and witches in North America, the Atheopagan ritual I led after my workshop was an absolution ritual. I could have gone for something shallower: a simple Springtime celebration or welcoming and fellowship ritual. But I wanted to do something that would be personal even to a group of strangers. Something that would be of service to them. So I urged them to call forth an embarrassing or shameful memory, something that makes their chests crawl when they think about it (we all have them), and to hold that feeling.

And then, wearing the Mask of Compassion, I absolved them of these. Dipping my fingers in a chalice of rainwater and water from the Chalice Well at Glastonbury Tor in England, I drew three circles on the forehead of each celebrant, saying: "You are pure. You are absolved. You are clean. It's gone!", my hands raising open at the last phrase.

I'm sure there was a broad range of experiences among celebrants given the diversity of the group and the setting (a hotel suite), but several participants reported they had felt powerful shifts within them. It was a very short ritual among a roomful of total strangers, but they nonetheless felt something of value.

My point here is that even under the most difficult of conditions, rituals that touch people and real healing work can be done. It's worth taking the risk of going deep.

3. Where to Do Rituals?

Safety and privacy are preeminent considerations in choosing a setting for a ritual. A location where a ritual may be interrupted or where passers by may be able to observe the festivities can make it hard for celebrants to enter the Ritual State. In some cases, a person may have to be designated as a Ward, to prevent nonparticipants from coming within view of the ritual. And take it from me: don't circle on someone else's private property without their permission. Not only is it rude and possibly dangerous, your celebrants will spend the entire ritual looking over their shoulders to see if the owner is coming, and will not be able to enter the Ritual State.

Doing rituals outdoors in Nature feels wonderful, but it is not always practical. When working indoors, it becomes that much more important to use effective ritual techniques to help celebrants to achieve the Ritual State.

Nature presents its own challenges. Without walls and a ceiling to reverberate from, sound tends to disappear. Wind and temperature can create conditions ranging from simply annoying to completely impossible for certain kinds of rituals. I attended a ritual on the beach once where we were to write down something we were ready to let go of, and put it in the fire. Unfortunately, it was so windy that many of us ended up ritually casting our wishes into the wind and the dune grass instead of the fire...not to mention that our "circle" became a horseshoe as celebrants avoided the column of smoke pouring sharply to one side.

Develop experience working in different environments. Be sure always to think through the logistics of what you are planning: if an important part of the ritual is to light a candle, what if there is a high wind? Is there an alternative that will fulfill the same function?

4. INGREDIENTS: Core concepts and elements for successful ritual

Authenticity is the felt sense that what is happening in the ritual is true and genuine rather than contrived or insincere. It is critically important to successful ritual—think of how easy it is to become detached and cynical when listening, for example, to the obviously insincere abjurations of a televangelist.

It is far better to speak briefly and from the heart in plain language than to read something lengthier that is written. While I won't say that rituals should never involve words that are read from paper or index cards, such presentation lacks the immediacy, authenticity and sense of *spontaneous creation* that are the desirable qualities in a ritual. Ritual is a living art, not a recital: it is about filling with richness the ephemeral moments within which it is created. If it is considered important that specific words be spoken, it is best if who must speak them memorize them and are able to present them as if spoken off the cuff.

Be careful, too, to avoid trite or excessively flowery speech: while poetic rhythms and imagery can be powerful, language that is obviously trying to be "poetic-seeming" fails more often than it succeeds. Modern people don't generally respond well to "thees" and "thous" or verse forced into rhyme schemes through awkward sentence construction; far better to speak normally in free verse, or simply as you would in a conversation.

Awe, Humility and Reverence are touchstone emotions for Atheopagan rituals and central to our view of the world. Although we do not worship, we know how small, temporary and precious are our lives, and how mighty, amazing and beautiful is the great Cosmos which gave rise to us. Honoring the Cosmos and the Earth are common aspects of our rituals which touch on a great truth of our existence of humans, and our practice as Atheopagans.

Being in the Body. Ritual is most effective when it engages not only the mind, but the body. Dance, movement, drumming or shaking a rattle, and singing all tend to bring the entire body into the experience of ritual and make ritual more satisfying and meaningful. Singing, particularly, is effective because it combines artistic expression with deep breathing, which enlivens the body through elevated oxygen and serotonin levels.

Creativity. Many effective rituals ask that participants bring something with them, do something to transform, imbue with meaning, or otherwise use that something in the ritual, and then take it home with them—perhaps charged to do yet something else with it when they go home. Various kinds of simple craft projects can make wonderful ritual activities, especially if they can be made collaboratively with others in the ritual. Artistic creation is inherently present and inherently self-affirming—it is an expression of the inner life of the creator and will lend personal significance and emotional power to a ritual.

Entrainment means *synchronization of participants with an external rhythm*, and it is accomplished through *repetition*. Drumming and rattling are common means to the entrainment of a group creating a ritual. In a broader sense, however, entrainment means getting all participants "on the same page", or moving in the same direction: to create a shared state in which they can express, celebrate and act together. Entrainment is a critically important aspect of successful ritual; when true entrainment has happened, you can feel that the ritual is really cooking.

Establishing Connection. Often, those who gather for a ritual may not all know one another. Even if they do, re-establishing their individual connections helps to establish Presence, let down defenses and "set the table" for a successful ritual. Examples of common activities to encourage connection early on in rituals include having participants join hands, look into eyes of those adjacent or all around the circle, and/or exchange of an "icebreaker" introduction question or activity.

Grounding is a process which can help to instill both *Presence* and *being in the body*. Grounding uses *guided imagery meditation*, where a ritual participant talks the rest of the participants through a meditation "story" in which they become aware of their bodies, of the pressure of their feet against the Earth, of the physicality of where they are and that they are physical beings. Grounding is very commonly performed at or before the formal beginning of a ritual to help begin the process of arrival in ritual Presence.

Group Participation and Ritual Etiquette are a right and a responsibility. Rituals work best when many participants contribute to their content with music, spoken word, or other contributions. It is the responsibility of a participant to pick carefully her moment to come forward with an offering, and avoid stepping on someone else's. Don't hog the focus for too long. Be present and pay attention to others when they are offering something. Know that there will be a moment for you, and wait for it to come.

Metaphor and the Poetic. Songs and spoken poetry can be profoundly moving in a ritual context. Poetry uses language in unexpected ways that tend to disconnect the cognitive mind and stir the emotions, and metaphor and symbolic allusions to meaningful concepts raise the spirits and can evoke contemplation of the stipulated theme, awe, humility and reverence.

No Spectators—All Participants. Atheopagan rituals are collaborative in nature. A ritual in which some are the "doers" and the rest observers is not going to feel very good to those in the latter category. Engaging all participants somehow—even if only by shaking a rattle or clapping their hands—is essential for the process of entrainment and in creating the feeling that all are participants. Make sure that there is a role for everyone—something s/he will do that contributes to the ritual's success: join in a song, drum or rattle along with a simple beat, perform a craft activity, dance in a circle holding hands with others, etc.

Presence. The key quality of effective ritual is that it brings the participant into the *meaningful present*, as opposed to thinking about the past or the future, feeling self-conscious or worried. The felt sense of this state is a glowing, aware feeling of well-being, similar to the state of creating art or deep human interaction. Presence needs not always be quiet or internal: Presence can range from the hushed sense of holiness felt in a magnificent cathedral to the ecstatic joy of wild dancing, or keening grief. From a neurochemical standpoint, it is the experience of high levels of serotonin and dopamine: the activation of the limbic brain. It is also sometimes known as the *Ritual State.*

Structure is the order of phases or events in a ritual. Structure is useful because once learned, participants know what to expect and are thus more able to "lose themselves" in the moment of the ritual. Not all rituals are firmly structured. See p. 8 for an example of an Atheopagan ritual structure.

Theme is the intended purpose of a ritual. Often this is the celebration of a particular season or life event, but a theme may also be to align the participants with a hoped-for outcome, such as finding a good job or recovering from an illness. The theme determines what symbols, metaphors and symbolic acts will be incorporated into the ritual to imbue it with the desired meaning and emotional impact.

5. Ritual Techniques and Technologies

Ritual techniques (also sometimes referred to as "ritual technologies") are sensory techniques which are used to help participants enter and stay in the state of ritual Presence. Effective rituals appeal to many senses at once, creating an *immersive* experience which facilitates participants' transition into the Limbic state: into Presence. To identify techniques which are effective in this, we need only look to traditions which have spent millennia refining their ritual techniques, like ancient sects of Buddhism or the Roman Catholic Church. In their rituals and temples, they use some or all of these techniques:

Dim lighting. Flickering candlelight or firelight is best. Low light contributes to a quieter, more meditative state and helps to support a sense of anonymity, enabling ritual participants to feel freer to express themselves. Firelight in particular appears to have a biologically hardwired attractiveness for humans: people will gravitate to a fire whenever they see one, much as they do to churning water such as a waterfall or the ocean.

Aesthetic and symbolism-laden beauty embodied in such forms as stained glass, magnificent architecture, icons, ritual tools and altars contributes to a sense of joy and pleasure in living, as well as evoking the metaphors and symbols of the religion's mythology. In an Atheopagan context, this might mean images of nature, stars or a galaxy, seasonal symbols, beautiful rocks, shells, feathers, and even scientific symbols or instruments. The author, for example, keeps a Moebius strip on his Focus (see below), as a reminder of the surprising and wonderful mathematical nature of the Universe.

Rhythm and rhythmic repetition such as drumming, rattling, chanting or playing of bells is the most effective way to establish entrainment for participants in a ritual. Rhythm speaks directly to the body, encouraging expressive movement and with it, a sense of being in the body and physically enlivened. Repetition of acts, words or activities in rituals tends to make them feel more effective and "real". This has been scientifically verified and appears to be linked to cognitive association of cause and effect: that is, we tend to believe that doing "more" of something makes it happen "more". http://www.sciencedaily.com/releases/2012/07/120726135234.htm

Singing and chanting (often combined with rhythm and/or in languages unknown to participants, and thus effectively nonsense syllables) Beautiful ore compelling music, as well as singing by participants (often with rhythmic repetition of phrases or melodies) is powerfully influential over the emotions and can transport ritual participants into a trance state. Much of the most emotionally powerful sung music in the world was originally composed for religious services.

Movement and dance, especially repetitive dance and

movement in a circle, contributes deeply to Presence and being in the body. While this may seem to be a strange idea for those accustomed to Judeo-Christian "leader and audience" ritual formats, most cultures in the world have celebrated their religions with movement as well as the other technologies described here, from the ecstatic ritual dances of the Hindus to the "whirling Mevlevi" (dervishes) of Sufism.

Scents such as incense and sacred oils can help to bring participants into Presence and a feeling of being in sacred space. "Smoke blessing" participants with smoke is an effective way to help them feel transformed as they enter the ritual experience, and is often done with incense, burning sage, sweetgrass or oak leaves. Scent is a powerfully evocative sense with a profound ability to alter mood; traditional religious incenses such as copal and frankincense have even been shown to alleviate depression and anxiety (http://www.sciencedaily.com/releases/2008/05/080520110415.htm)

Similarly, the **taste** of food and drink consumed during a ritual—such as bread and wine, a ritual meal such as a Passover Seder, etc.—can enhance Presence while also evoking a sense of religious tradition and continuity: of having done the same ritual at previous times. The circulation of "cakes and ale"—which can mean any kind of drink and finger food—is a common element of Pagan rituals, and usually takes place during the Gratitude portion of Atheopagan rites.

Touch and tactile experiences are very powerful and

contribute to participants' inhabiting their senses and being in the body, especially when the sensations come as a surprise, as when the eyes are closed or in full darkness. I have seen tactile experiences used in ritual ranging from the sharp patter of water droplets from "asperging" with a water sprinkler to passage of soft fur across the face, passage of a chunk of ice from hand to hand, cloths damp with hot water given to each participant to cleanse the face, etc.

6. The Focus (altar)

A *Focus* is what Atheopagans call an altar. We choose a different word because "altar" implies worship—or even sacrifice—and we want to be clear that that isn't what we are doing.

The Focus is:

A curated collection of meaningful objects gathered together for ritual use and placed upon one or more surfaces in an intentional pattern.

The Focus is a work of art, a still life assemblage of symbols and meaningful objects. It can be central to the enactment of a ritual, or it may be off to one side. Multiple Focuses may be used if desired, designed around different themes. Building a Focus is a fun and creative activity and can itself be done as a ritual, in an intentional, Present and "focused" manner.

Typically, a Focus incorporates multiple elements of ritual technology: candles, incense, symbolic items, art, food items to be shared and/or items to be used during the ritual, etc. The creation of a Focus is a subtle art. A successful one will draw the eye and evoke fascination and curiosity when first viewed.

When building one, be sure to remember that you will need lighting of some kind if the ritual will take place under low lighting conditions: candles or oil lamps are the warmest and most welcoming light. *Always remember fire safety.*

These objects may be of practical use in a ritual, or chosen solely for their symbolic meaning to the person or people creating the Focus. A Focus may be built anywhere with horizontal surfaces on which to place the objects: a shelf, a table, a mantle, a tree stump, or simply the ground. Often, the Focus is constructed atop a cloth or other covering draped over the surface(s) on which it is built.

When building a Focus, here are some considerations:

Themes: Is this Focus a temporary one for a particular ritual on a particular theme? You will want symbols that go with that theme, then. If you're building a more per-manent personal Focus, consider all the most important themes to you. For example, my Focus at home has elements devoted to natural beauty, to my friends, to sexuality, to ancestry, to the Beloved Dead, and to evolution. So ask yourself: *what's important to me?* What do I really need represented on my Focus to capture my character, values and aspirations?

Aesthetics: The Focus should delight the eye and intrigue and draw in the viewer. Beauty matters! What colors are consistent with the theme? What symbols? You might use symbols of the Earth, Sun and Moon, fresh flowers, beautiful objects from nature, artworks consistent with the Focus themes, etc. Arrange them attractively! If there is a wall behind the Focus surface, you can mount images and artworks on it.

What ritual tools do you regularly use? Common examples include candles or oil lamps, chalices, knives, wands, incense burners, Tarot decks, jewelry that is only worn during rituals, an Atheopagan Rosary, or other such practical ritual tools. Many Atheopagans who come from the Pagan tradition may have more of these "occult"-style tools, but they aren't *necessary*–they just add some color and "Oooooo!" factor to a ritual.

Practical considerations: If you're going to serve wine in a chalice, do you have a corkscrew? (Alternatively, it can be opened early and the cork partially replaced until needed). How about a chalice to pass, or cups? If the ritual is to take place in darkness, are there candles or other lights to illuminate the Focus so its beauty and meaning can be seen? If you intend to burn incense, do you have a source of fire to light it? If you will asperge (sprinkle) participants with water as a tactile experience for bringing them into their senses and Presence, do you have something to dip in the water and shake at each participant (a sprig of rosemary is nice)? Less attractive practical considerations like matches and extra incense can be stored behind or to the side of the Focus, or in an attractive container such as a wooden box. And do you have a way to put out a fire, just in case?

Finally, once you have created your personal Focus, *keep it "alive"*. Meaning, don't just let it sit. Make it a site of change and activity. Light the candles and/or burn incense regularly. Move things around. Change it with the changing of the seasons. Clean the Focus occasionally to keep dust from accumulating. Speak a short intention or blessing at your Focus each morning before leaving the house.

My Focus is the literal focus of religious activity and observance in my home. It is a comfort to me to see it when I come home, and contemplating its symbols and glowing candles makes it easy for me to enter the Present, liminal Ritual State, or "trance".

May your Focuses be as richly satisfying!

7. Ritual Hygiene and Taking Care of Yourself

Depending on their contents, rituals can be physically taxing. They can work up your feelings and metabolic and heart rates, and simply attaining and being in the Ritual State of focus, presence, emotion and awareness can burn a lot of calories.

Accordingly, we need to take care of our bodies and our minds prior to and following a ritual.

Pre-Arrival phase: Generally speaking, it is good to prepare for a ritual by eating a light, healthy snack of some kind, like a piece of fruit, and ensuring that you are sufficiently hydrated. Get a good night of sleep the night before if at all possible.

There are exceptions to these rules. Sometimes fasting is employed in the lead-up to a ritual, or sleep deprivation, or both. These can contribute to a ritual being very powerful, but are also dangerous unless thorough grounding and return to a normal state are employed after the ritual's closing.

Hydration is *always* a must. Have water available for participants during a ritual and be sure you are sipping water, whether or not you feel you need it.

Post-Benediction phase: After a ritual, you may find yourself feeling lightheaded or dreamy, still in the Ritual State, or you may have had a profound emotional experience that is still lingering with you. The limbic system of the brain is highly activated during the Ritual State; this creates an altered state of consciousness which can be dangerous when it comes to engaging with physical reality: do not, for example, jump right in a car and drive while in this state.

Instead, do what you can to "ground" or re-orient your body and mind to an ordinary state of consciousness.

Eat something hearty. Touch the soles of your feet or your bare palms flat against the Earth and just breathe for a few minutes, concentrating on your breath going in and out. Then sit quietly and just notice your surroundings: pay particular attention to their details. Soon, you will feel more "normal" and will be able to go about the business of cleaning up from the ritual and moving on with your day or night.

The Ritual State is pleasurable and powerful, but it is also an altered state of consciousness and should not be combined with operating heavy machinery or other dangerous activities. Be sure to take care of yourself as you conduct your ritual work.

8. An Atheopagan Ritual Format

The format below is not the only possible structure for an Atheopagan ritual; indeed, there are as many possible ways of doing ritual as there are individual practitioners. But this is a format that I have been successful in using for effective Atheopagan rituals, and it is the structure I use as a standard practice.

It has six phases:

Arrival. Establishment of Presence and entrainment; "grounding" to shake off prior irritations and worries about the future. Establishment of ritual space—some may do this by "drawing a circle" around the proceedings, but this is a matter of taste.

Qualities. A participatory phase wherein participants may call out, sing, invoke with movement or poetry, etc., those qualities they wish to be in the minds of the participants as part of the "mixture" created by the ritual.

Intentions. Sometimes the Intentions of a given ritual are stipulated in advance as a Theme (e.g., seasonal celebration, wedding, prosperity ritual, etc.); at other times, participants may call out or otherwise introduce their wishes for the outcome of the ritual: to align themselves with a particular outcome or "program" their minds with a particular attitude, for example.

Deep Play or "Working". The hardest section to define, because it can be anything that brings the inner child out to play in meaningful celebration, be it singing, dancing, collaboration on a project, improvisational harmony or rhythm, etc. Whatever it is, this section is about *being alive* in the experience of the moment, and celebrating that living and the others who share it with you. The activity can be themed around the Intentions set earlier, may involve a particular craft activity or creation of a ritual object, or the Deep Play can be more free-form, with participants spontaneously offering songs or poems, inviting others to join them in drumming or dancing or other activity, etc. Generally speaking there is an effort to rev up the metabolism, to stimulate the body so there is a feeling of energy and vitality, but sometimes it can be a mental journey of guided imagery or other more tranquil activity. If there is a time limitation, the time to end Deep Play may be signaled by a bell or other auditory cue.

Gratitude. When Deep Play has wound down, it is time to give thanks for all the many blessings we enjoy. Participants name their gratitudes, and often, food and drink are shared as a reminder that the world feeds us delicious (and sometimes intoxicating) gifts.

Benediction. A "farewell" which indicates that the ritual is over, typically with good wishes for the participants and their aspirations, and humanity in general. Usually articulated by whoever convened or organized the ritual, or simply assigned to someone.

9. Exploring the Phases of the Atheopagan Ritual Format

A. Arrival

The goal of *Arrival is induction into the Ritual State*: a liminal "glowing" feeling of acute sensory awareness in the present moment, and of deep connection with both participants in the ritual and the broader Universe. Physiologically, the Ritual State is characterized by elevated levels of the neurotransmitters serotonin and dopamine, and higher activation of the Limbic brain than is usual. The process of induction into the Ritual State shares many similarities to induction into a state of hypnosis or trance. It feels great: alert, powerful, calm and highly Present.

The Arrival phase of ritual is necessary because our quotidian mental state is quite different from the Ritual State. Challenges to be overcome by the Arrival phase include *preoccupation* (thinking about the past or future), *self-consciousness /cynicism* (feeling embarrassed by or resistant to the prospect of entering the Ritual State), and *self-containment* (feeling separate from other participants, and uncomfortable with opening to them emotionally).

The practices in the Arrival phase are designed to calm these effects and shift consciousness into preparedness for ritual work.

Arrival has several components, all or only some of which may be used in a given ritual. Not every ritual uses all of them, but they are most effective when performed in the order shown.

Establishing the Space. Create a setting conducive to the Ritual State by using <u>lighting</u> (firelight or candlelight are best—flickering and dim—but low light levels with Christmas lights or rope lights can also create a good light level. Overhead light is not advised[1]); <u>scent</u>(resinous incenses such as frankincense and dragon's blood are particularly effective); <u>Focus(es)</u> (i.e., altar(s)) with visual cues that draw the eye and communicate meanings; and sometimes <u>music </u>(when I do solitary ritual, I often put on recorded ritual music. My favorites are *Passion*, the soundtrack to the film "The Last Temptation of Christ", by Peter Gabriel; *In the Realm of a Dying Sun* and *The Serpent's Egg* by Dead Can Dance; Offerings, by Vas, and *Stratosfear,* by Tangerine Dream).

The ritual begins when setup begins, so be mindful as you place objects, light incense, etc. Be silent, speaking quietly only when necessary. Begin the process of centering within

---

1   Obviously, the use of lighting to affect setting and mood is for rituals held at night. Knowing that it can be more challenging for some celebrants to achieve the Ritual State in bright-light conditions, it is often helpful to use more Arrival techniques (e.g., smudging, grounding, embodiedness techniques) in daylight rituals.

yourself, of becoming Present yourself.

Entering the Now; Sudden stimulation of the senses can help celebrants to inhabit their senses and aid them in becoming Present. Examples of techniques in this category are *smudging* (wafting or fanning smoke over each celebrant) with burning herbs or incense; *asperging* (sprinkling each celebrant) with water or scented water; use of a chime, singing bowl, rattle, didjeridoo or other instrument to outline the body in a *sound blessing*; or administration of a *sacramental taste* of something flavorful—a single dark chocolate chip, for example, or a drop of sour cherry on the tongue—to draw each participant's consciousness into the senses, into the present, into the sacred Now.

Creating Connection is intended to break the sense of "social boundary" between celebrants. Example techniques including having celebrants hold hands, make eye contact with one another around the ritual circle, or each speak her/his name. Connection (in group rituals) is important because it establishes a greater sense of safety than otherwise, improving the ability of celebrants to surrender into the Ritual State.

Grounding is in most cases the use of guided imagery by spoken word to connect the celebrant with where she is in time and space, and to remind her of the vastness and beauty of the great Cosmos and of the living Earth. It is often helpful to coordinate this with awareness of breathing, as in mindfulness and meditation practices. Grounding can be enhanced physically by such actions as standing with bare feet upon the Earth or holding a heavy stone.

Embodiment is expansion of the felt sense of the Ritual State to encompass the body. Techniques to achieve embodiment include musical activities such as toning or singing or a heartbeat drum (which results in swaying, slow movement), or upbeat drumming/music to provoke more active dancing. Bluesy/gospely chants and songs work well for embodiment.

After these steps, all or most participants will be in ritual Presence and ready to do ritual work. It is time to move into the next phase: **Qualities (Intentions).**

B. Invoking Qualities and (optionally) Intentions

"Calling the Qualities" is often just that: A designated celebrant encourages the circle to call out the Qualities they would like to be a part of the circle, and celebrants call them out (examples: the Ancestors; Compassion; Grief; Courage; Adventure, Strength, Health, Wisdom). It is more effective if, after each Quality is invoked, the remainder of the circle repeats the word or phrase.

This can be done in "popcorn" fashion or sequentially around the circle; it can be done singing, or even danced.

There are probably hundreds of creative ways the Qualities can be invoked.

In some rituals there may be preassigned participants to invoke particular Qualities with more detailed invocations, similar to "calling the quarters" in a Wiccan/Neopagan ritual. In fact, special Focuses may be built on the themes of these Qualities to evoke greater attention to them on the part of celebrants.

Note that if there is a particularly important Quality you want to be the central focus of the ritual, this should have a special invocation of its own.

C. Intentions (Optional)

Many rituals have their intentions determined in advance, or their purposes are self-evident: to celebrate a Sabbath, for example. In these cases, declaring the intention of the ritual is not necessary, although celebrants may choose to do so.

Some rituals do not have a clear and obvious intention, however, or may have multiple intentions. In the latter case, after the invocation of the Qualities, declaration of the intended effect of the ritual adds to the psychological power of the ritual, and allows participants to add their own personal goals to the ritual's "cauldron" if they so choose. A designated celebrant can declare the intention, or participants may be encouraged to call out their own.

After the Qualities have been invoked and the Intentions

have been established, it is time for the "meat" of the ritual: the **Deep Play,** sometimes also called the "working".

D. Deep Play or "Working"

Deep Play is the hardest phase to write about, because it can be nearly anything. It can be free-form dancing with spontaneously offered chant, song, spoken word, and music, or line or spiral dancing; it can be laying of hands on an ailing celebrant; it can be shared harmonic improvisational singing; it can be weaving together or braiding of strands of yarn representing Qualities to be integrated while singing a chant; it can be the passing of a mirror from hand to hand as each celebrant contemplates his reflection to the sound of a heartbeat drum; it may be drumming and singing while each celebrant in turn makes an offering or performs an action.

In short, it can be anything that enacts symbolic and/or literal implementation of the *transformative work* of the ritual.

Typically, that activity will:

Stimulate, whether metabolically or contemplatively. Pulsing drumming, soaring harmonies, or calming/entrancing sounds like singing bells, tinkling chimes, or a quiet flute can set the emotional tone for celebrants while they are conducting the ritual's Deep Work activity.

Communicate Meaning, in the sense that what is done in Deep Play is freighted with metaphorical or symbol meaning beyond simple carrying out of an action.

Preserve the Ritual State. It is critically important that whatever activities take place in the circle during Deep Play must be tailored to aid celebrants in maintaining their Ritual State—their condition of open, empowered Presence. Even in lighthearted ritual, there is an underlying seriousness to the work that must be honored. So while stimulation is key, too much stimulation or the wrong emotional tone can "break the spell". Imagine the Ritual State, the "energy" of a ritual as a soap bubble which must be kept aloft without breaking.

Some Deep Play is designed to increase in energy and build to a climax; some to remain at a "steady boil" rather than to climb. Some may even rise and then fall, to the point that at its end, there is only a whisper of activity, and then silence. All are effective ways to work with the emotional feeling of Deep Play, and may be selected for usage when appropriate.

The potential palette of activities and emotional flavors of Deep Play is nearly infinite. This phase of ritual is where much of the opportunity for creativity and imagination in ritual design is found.

When Deep Play is completed—when all participants have completed its activity, the energy has climbed to a climax or dwindled to a murmur—it is time to begin the dénouement of the ritual: **Gratitude** and **Benediction.**

E. Gratitude

When the Deep Play is done, it is time to express Gratitude. Gratitude is such a key element of a happy life that even when our rituals are to assuage fear or sorrow, we must always remember the many gifts with which we are showered by the Cosmos every day.

Gratitude is often done in a manner similar to Invoking the Qualities, creating a kind of "bookend" effect: either going around the circle and having each celebrant express what s/he is grateful for, or doing so in random "popcorn" fashion. Celebrants may also express gratitude that the Qualities were with them in the circle, e.g., "I am thankful that Discipline is with me, and supports the work I do here."

Gratitude is often combined with the sharing of ceremonial food and drink—a way for participants to feel their very bodies surging with gratitude as, say, a rich red wine or ripe strawberry or chocolate or freshly baked bread encounters their taste buds. We are alive today, says the phase of Gratitude: thank you for this, and for those who love us, and for all the great and small blessings we enjoy in this precious life we live.

F. Benediction

Benediction is the formal ending of the ritual: an expression of well-wishing and encouragement that celebrants act in accordance with the intentions of the ritual.

I prefer to end my rituals the same way each time, in the hope that my co-celebrants will learn this benediction in the same way so many Pagans have learned the "all from air into air, let the misty curtains part…" closing statement so commonly used in Wiccan-style rituals.

My usual benediction is this:

"To enrich and honor the gift of our lives, to chart a kind and true way forward, by these words and deeds we name intent (participants join in unison): to dare, to question, to love. May all that must be done, be done in joy. We go forth to live!"

Sometimes after the Benediction, a closing song is sung by celebrants—this can be a wonderful and connecting way to complete the ritual process.

No Hierarchy: Atheopagan Leadership

Note that nowhere in this work is there any suggestion of hierarchical levels or "priest/esses". As I choose to practice my Atheopagan religion, there are none. While a particular person might take on responsibility for organizing or designing a given ritual, no Atheopagan participant is higher in status or standing than any other.

It's a sadly familiar tale in the Pagan community: the coven or local organization that is run by a charismatic "high priestess" or "high priest" (or both), doling out "training" and "degrees of advancement" based on how well the subject toes the line, fawns over the "priest/ess", and, in some particularly sad cases, provides them with sexual favors as a part of the "initiatory process".

Or…the narcissistic Pagan "leader" who works to cultivate a young and pretty entourage of on-tap adorers as a part of imparting their "wisdom" to followers…and for whom those not so young or pretty never quite seem to make the grade for advancement.

Or…the dirty secret that eventually comes out about some bright and innocent aspiring newby who ends up being harassed until driven away by such a "leader".

But wait…isn't that essentially the sad and common story in pretty much every religious community?

I'll cut to the chase: that entire model—of hierarchy in power, respect and even obedience in spiritual community—is rotten to its core. It is a guaranteed formula for abuse. It is the same as when bosses have power over employees, when teachers have power over students, and when adults have power over children. And while those power gradients may be inevitable, we don't have to have them in religion.

We see it in the Christians, we see it in the Buddhists, we see it in the Pagans. Doesn't matter the cosmology and practice. Having some people who are considered "more advanced and important" in a religious context just doesn't keep people safe.

I don't know how many times I have heard from bright, creative, interesting, wise people that they gave up on their local Pagan community because of some would-be guru abusing the trust that others placed in them: socially, financially, sexually.

I've seen it myself, close up.

And as far as I'm concerned, in Atheopaganism we ain't doing that.

Yes, I'm the primary voice at Atheopaganism.org, and on the Facebook Atheopaganism group. And mine is the name most associated with this path, because I started it and I'm devoting a significant chunk of my life to helping to build and raise the visibility of its vision and practices.

But I am NOT the high priest of the Atheopagans. We have no clergy, no advancement levels. I'm just a guy with ideas who cares, devoting what skills and wisdom he has to making a path. Others seem to find it valuable, and that's really gratifying to me: it makes me feel committed to the Atheopagan community, to feel love and inspiration that these ideas and practices are of value in the lives of others.

YOU, person reading this, are the "high priest/ess" of your life. You are the ultimate moral authority in relation to you. Given learning of ritual skills and a desire to do so, you can be the leader of a ritual just as well as anyone. And you have as much standing to contribute lore, philosophy, and suggested practices to Atheopaganism as anyone else.

If you find something in what I write objectionable, I hope you will communicate that directly to me. Let's talk about it. Maybe I got something wrong, or have a blind spot. Or maybe you just have a better idea for how to handle a particular situation or ritual technique. Bring it forth! We are collaborating in building this path together.

Some of the stories that have come forward in the wake of the abuse accusations against Pagan "leaders" online have nearly brought me to tears, because they are from good people who were driven out of Pagan community by the sheer dysfunction of those who claimed to be its leading exponents. I've seen it myself, in a Pagan organization where grounded and sensible and functional people would come in, look around, and run screaming...but crazy and creepy settled in and stayed for years.

One of the truly wonderful things about creating a new tradition is that we can learn from the mistakes of those who have gone before us. And in Atheopaganism, I'm doing my best not to introduce any element that can be distorted or abused to enable the kinds of shenanigans described above.

There is an anarchist slogan: No gods. No masters. This has been adapted by some theistic Pagans to Many gods. No masters.

Well, I'm here to tell you, folks, if you have a priesthood standing at a level between you and your gods—if you really think that someone who calls themselves a "priestess of Goddess X" has a closer relationship with that aspect of the Sacred than you do—you've got masters, whether you want them or not. And some of them will inevitably betray you.

So I say *No gods. No masters. No priests. No priestesses.*

Just we critters, equal and humble under the gaze of the Sun, working together to make our way.

Atheopaganism and Activism

People's relationships with the world of public policy, elections and world affairs vary widely. For some, they are background noise, irrelevant distractions to the matters of their own lives, beliefs and practices.

There are many Pagans like this. While they may espouse political opinions or share memes on Facebook, they're not doing much to change the world through political or activism channels. Some of them don't even vote, expressing the bizarre idea that by refusing to take a stand in an election, they are somehow taking a more important stand in a larger context. (Personally, I don't get it. I don't see how one can believe that doing nothing is doing anything but endorsing things as they are. Myself, I'll take every tool available, thanks very much.)

Atheopagans are practical people. We understand that the world is real, and finite, and that its systems are fragile. We respect science and listen to its warnings. We know that there are no gods or magical processes which are going to bail us out from the inevitable results of our actions here on Earth. Nor is there an afterlife to save our bacon if we make the Earth uninhabitable.

So *is* Atheopaganism political? I believe it certainly is. I don't see how one can be in this world, at this time, with Atheopagan values and not feel a deep call to action.

Atheopaganism is about unflinching attention to what is most likely to be *TRUE*: the usage of critical thinking, science and evidence-based analysis to draw the most rea-sonable conclusions from the available data. Anyone using such an approach can clearly see that we are in dire times. Times which confront our species with threats such as it has never seen before.

In times like these, I believe it is our moral obligation not only to revere what is sacred—Life, Truth, Beauty, Love—but to act in a manner that increases the odds of these persisting in the future. In my particular case, that has meant a lot of grassroots organizing, electoral politics and lobbying.

But that's only one channel: consumer choices are deeply important as well. Other than consumables like food, I buy nearly nothing new; with a little effort, one can dress well and even professionally with used clothes exclusively. Nor do I find the need to consume much *stuff*. I've felt I have more than enough stuff for many years now. Even when I replace my phone—when the old one dies—I choose a dated model which is no longer in production from my provider, or I buy a used replacement.

Litigation has its place; direct action to protect resourc-es and build public attention until institutions that hold power can be convinced to reverse destructive decisions has its place as well. And while I am deeply skeptical of its ability to gain any serious traction, hacking away at the roots of capitalism itself–through creation of alternative models, organizing shareholders, and direct action–also holds a place in this "ecosystem of activism".

Some of these activities may seem more like feelgood

gestures than powerful strategies to change what happens to the ecological webs of the Earth. But that doesn't matter. At this point a kitchen sink strategy is required. We must vote, we must organize, we must lobby, we must obstruct, we must educate, we must *implement through action our love of the world.*

Regrettably, in this country our political parties have so polarized that only one of the two real parties—by which, I mean the parties that can actually attain power, rather than going through the motions as also-rans—is EVER the right choice when it comes to caring about the Earth, about supporting love in all its forms, about advancing principles of justice and equality, about making decisions based on what is true rather than ideological nonsense. That is the Democratic Party, obviously. It certainly has its flaws, but so does everything else that exists in the real world.

We're not here to hold our breaths waiting for unicorns and magic bullets we can endorse with wild enthusiasm. We're here to make things better, even if only by a little bit, with every volitional action we take. Once we've elected someone with more or less decent values, it's on us to ride that person with our committed and concerted voices to ensure they do the right thing. And if they fail us once in awhile, it's on us to understand that no one is perfect, nor can anyone be expected to be. There is a technical term in the political world for tossing in the dumpster someone who is with you 90% of the time because of the other 10%: "suicide".

Does the urgency of the situation mean that we should give up on such approaches as "too slow"? No, I'm afraid not. Because if positive change at a broad scale is going to happen, it is going to happen as a result of decisions made within the channels of power. It is going to happen because those channels have chosen for it to happen. And that means we need to show up, keep the pressure on and make it so. It is a pleasant fantasy to believe that "if the people just rise up" all wrongs can be righted, but the truth of the world is that some people have more power than others, and they must be cajoled, wrangled, and cornered into doing the right thing, if it is to be done at all.

I worked in politics on behalf of the environment for a long time. I'm a bit more removed now, but the organization I work for now has direct beneficial impact both on the environment and on local communities, and that matters a lot in my book.

Not everyone is going to devote their career to the Earth as I have, but everyone can *do something*. Write a letter to the editor. Register people to vote. Volunteer for a campaign. Call your local, state and federal representatives—don't be intimidated, they work for *us*.

Go to a demonstration. Lead a boycott. Volunteer for a phonebank. Work a precinct. Donate.

But do something. Say something. *Take action.*

In the name of Life, and Love, and Truth, and Beauty, let it be so.

Recently, I've been seeing a lot of postings in Pagan groups on Facebook in which posters advocate for "spellwork", "hexes", "bindings" and other so-called "spiritual activism", with the goal that these will influence the current state of public affairs, such as the many disastrous policies of the U.S. Trump administration.

Sorry, folks, but that's not activism. It may make you *feel* as though you are doing something, but you're not. And therein lies its danger.

Now, I think that rituals for activists are great. They can help to support, motivate, focus and encourage us as we work to create a better world. At the 2017 Pantheacon, I was a presenter of "Arming the Warriors of the Earth: An Activist's Ritual", which was all about empowering those who commit themselves to public benefit advocacy.

But that doesn't mean that holding a ritual is going to affect things all by itself.

Our values as Atheopagans advocate for a better, kinder, more ecologically responsible world. And for that world to come requires physical, material-world action…and *not* just symbolic, ritual action.

We must communicate with decision makers—often, politely, and with clarity about what we want. We must vote, and volunteer to organize voters. We must write letters to the editor, and talk with our friends. We must speak out against bigotry and injustice. We must run for office ourselves. We must support the organizations that are
doing the heavy lifting in advocating for our values. We

must march. We must spend our money where it does good, or at least less harm.

We must be voices for what we want to see in the world.

So certainly: light that candle and speak that invocation for peace and kindness. But then get on the phone and let your representatives know exactly what you expect from them. Write a letter. Join a phone bank. Volunteer for a weekend canvass.

And vote. **Vote, vote, vote.**

Do something real and tangible to advocate for a better world.

You'll be surprised at how good it feels. And as millions upon millions act, how much change can be made.

SUNTREE:
The Significance of the Atheopagan Symbol

In summer of 2018, the Atheopagan community went through a process of selecting a symbol for our path. Many designs were submitted, and after several rounds of voting, we settled on the above: the **Suntree.**

I've been wearing a Suntree ever since. I get compliments on it often—it's a friendly design, apparently, and I'm not the only one to think so.

I've found new meanings in the Suntree since we chose it—happy coincidences, if you will, or apophenia (seeing meaningful patterns where they were never intended, which, as we have discussed is a major perceptual foible of our human brains).

But they make me happy, and I thought I'd share them.

First, there is the green tree of the Earth and the golden rays of the Sun: the two most significant presences in our lives. I love that our symbol embodies the Sacred Earth and Cosmos, the Great Below and the Great Above.

Next, there are the numbers. The Sun has eight rays which equate to the eight Sabbaths of the Wheel of the Year. And when you add the five branches of the tree, you get 13: the number of Atheopagan Principles!

Of course, all of this is just pattern-projection onto a symbol for which few, if any of these meanings were originally intended. But that doesn't make the symbol any less meaningful for me. In fact, it kind of tickles me that the very phenomenon that leads people to believe in supernatural phenomena helps me to see meaning in our symbol.

I found it heartwarming to see so many people wearing Suntree buttons at Pantheacon (the largest indoor gathering of Pagans and witches in North America) in 2019, to smile in the hallways at each other, even if we didn't recognize one another otherwise.

Small as we are, we're a community and an identity, and we have a symbol that captures much of what we're about.

That makes me smile.

Various items, including neck pendants, with the Suntree symbol are available at The Atheopagan Store on Zazzle.com.

Conclusion: What It Looks Like

The perspective and practice described here can deliver the fulfillment benefits of a traditional religion, yet remain rooted in what is true and open to learning, change, and constant reconsideration of itself so it is not in danger of becoming ideological. While it does not make promises of eternal existence, a cosmically-determined plan leading to a "happy ending", or magical powers, it also does not ask us to sacrifice the unique and marvelous capacities of our Neocortical minds in the name of living with a pretty story.

I, for one, find this trade-off a worthy exchange.

Let's close with an invocation to the glory of the Universe.

An Atheopagan Prayer

Praise to the wide spinning world

Unfolding each of all the destined tales compressed
In the moment of your catastrophic birth

Wide to the fluid expanse, blowing outward

Kindling in stars and galaxies, in bright pools

Of Christmas-colored gas; cohering in marbles hot

And cold, ringed, round, gray and red and gold and dun

And blue, pure blue, the eye of a child, spinning in a veil of air,

Warm island, home to us, kind beyond measure: the stones

And trees, the round river flowing sky to deepest chasm,

Salt and sweet.

Praise to Time, enormous and precious,

And we with so little, seeing our world go as it will

Ruing, cheering, the treasured fading, precious arriving,
Fear and wonder,

Fear and wonder always.
Praise O black expanse of mostly nothing

Though you do not hear, you have no ear nor mind to hear

Praise O inevitable, O mysterious,

Praise and thanks be a wave

Expanding from this tiny temporary mouth

This tiny dot of world a bubble
A bubble going out forever

Meeting everything as it goes:

All the great and infinitesimal
Gracious and terrible
All the works of blessed Being.

May it be so.

May it be so.

May our hearts sing to say it is so.

Appendices

Organizing an Atheopagan Gathering
A planning guide

Introduction

While Atheopagans enjoy a variety of online communities, there is nothing like an in-person gathering to build lasting relationships, moving memories, and forward momentum in our movement. This planning guide is intended as a subject-by-subject walkthrough of the various phases of event planning so you can have a successful gathering of your own.

Concept and Goal Setting

To begin with, your event needs a concept. What is its intention? How many people do you hope to have attend? What are the outcomes you hope to achieve by the end of the event?

Most Atheopagan gatherings will have goals like ritual *experiences* and *community building*. But there can be others: to recruit the core of a regular ritual working group, for example, or even simply to make some money over and above expenses to offset the cost in time and effort for you, as the organizer.

So ask yourself: what am I trying to achieve here? How many people would make a good size for my event?

2) Planning and Timeline

I recommend that you start planning an event a full year in advance of its date. This allows for six months of logistics and planning, followed by six months of marketing, ticket sales, registration and development of programming.

The best way to plan an event is to work backwards from the production date, counting the number of days you need to perform various tasks. This is best handled using a spreadsheet.

3) Budgeting

In order for the event to succeed, it must at least pay for itself (unless you have outside underwriting).

An example budget spreadsheet can be downloaded at Atheopaganism.org.

Many Pagan events include a *scholarship fund* to help less affluent attendees to be able to come to them. Surplus funds can be used for this purpose, so think about how much money you really need to clear on the event in order to be able to ensure that all the people you would like to attend are able to come.

The budget provided at Atheopaganism.org shows a *sponsorship drive* as a part of its revenue. In a sponsorship drive, you approach supporters who have the means to give larger amounts to support your event, and ask them to contribute in exchange for recognition in the program and in person onsite. The suggested sponsorship levels given are $500 (which includes 4 tickets) and $250 (which includes 2 tickets), but you can adjust these as you see fit and according to your circumstances. Just remember that sponsorship should always bring in more than the value of the tickets that come with it.

Finally, some events include *advertising* in the paper program distributed at the registration table onsite. The program contains essential information about the event, such as the schedule of workshops and presentations, mealtimes, major underwriters such as sponsors, and the event's *conduct standards* (See "Policies", below). Advertising by local occult shops or bookstores can be a great way to pull in some more revenue for your event.

4) Choosing a venue

Good locations for Atheopagan gatherings have particular characteristics, and the three most important are nature, *travel distance* and a *fire circle*.

Ours is an Earth religion. When we gather to celebrate and build community, the most amenable place is not in an urban setting, but in a forest, or a desert, or mountains, or at the beach on a river, lake or ocean. Consider the beauty of a prospective site when choosing where to hold your event.

Another consideration is sound. Atheopagan rituals often

involve drumming and singing at night. Be sure to confirm that this will be okay with the owners of your prospective venue.

That said, it is also unreasonable to expect prospective attendees to travel a very long distance to reach your coming from far flung distances and are converging from many locations to your event, try to make your event easily accessible to them.

A circle within which one can light a fire and conduct a ritual is another necessity. People have been gathering around fires for hundreds of thousands of years; it is our natural ritual setting. Unless your venue has some other incredible ritual setting (like a system of caves, for example), having a place to light a fire and gather around it is necessary.

These two factors considered, logistics are critically important. A venue that is easy to reach, accessible for those with physical impairments, and which includes needed facilities is important. Kitchen facilities (or a place where a camp kitchen can be set up) and bathrooms are required, of course, and other amenities such as showers, a pool or a hot tub can all add to the enjoyment of your event.

Accessibility for the differently abled is an important consideration. If the venue is not easy to navigate for those in wheelchairs or using assistance to move around, you will have to have a plan for how to help such folk to get around to where they need to go.

5) Food

If possible, the easiest route is for attendees to bring their own food and do their own cooking, but in areas where there is fire danger or at some venues which require that attendees eat meals provided by the facility (easy, but expensive), this may not be possible.

Cooking for the group can be something that attendees do together (see "Community Service", below), or which can be taken on by a group of event staff who are either paid or comped for their admission. It can be fun and cohesion-building to cook together and clean up after each meal.

Sustainability tip: Have attendees bring their own plates, cups and utensils, and set up washing stations after each meal so they can wash their own. Usage of disposables really has no place in our religion.

Simple menu items that can still make for enjoyable meals must take into consideration that some people have dietary restrictions, so the best options are select-your-own buffets. Examples include:

BREAKFAST: Breakfast buffet with fruit, yogurt (serve from large container, not individual servings), bagels with toppings, hard boiled eggs, pastries or muffins, juices, coffee and tea. If possible, hot items can be added to these, such as scrambled eggs, bacon or sausages, pancakes or waffles.

LUNCH: Sandwich bar with many options, both vegetarian and omnivorous. Provide lettuce so lettuce wraps can be made by those avoiding gluten. Include sides such as green and potato salads and hummus.

DINNER: Taco bar with vegan taco "meat", vegetarian refried or black beans, sharp grated cheese, salsa, shredded lettuce, diced onions, sour cream, hot sauce and cilantro.

Another dinner option if a grill is available is a barbecue night with side dishes. There are many vegan/vegetarian options which can be grilled on their own section of the barbecue away from meats. Even organic chicken is quite affordable for the meat-eaters.

These are low-cost options which are tasty and filling and enable people to customize their food to their tastes. If more money is available, more expensive options can of course be offered.

6) Programming

Programming is—besides the socializing, of course!—what attendees are coming for. It includes workshops, rituals, performances, and whatever else is on the formal schedule of your event.

Here are some examples of programming that has been on the program of events I have organized or attended:

Opening circle

Bardic circle (where participants share songs, poems, stories and other creative works)

Workshops, such as on drumming, singing, dancing, and ritual design

Discussion panels

Musical performances

Ritual planning circle (to plan a ritual later in the event)

Main ritual

Closing circle.

So...how do you get programming?

You invite proposals.

When you announce your event, make sure that you contact those whose content you would like to feature. Let them know that you welcome submissions for presenting at your event, how long the presentation slots will be, and any other pertinent information about the event and what you're looking for in programming.

Give applicants a month or more to perfect and submit their proposals. Then you can review them and select those you want to invite. Be sure to notify selectees as soon as possible so they have plenty of time for preparing their presentations.

If you can afford to, it is sometimes helpful to cover the

entrance fee for presenters, so they're more likely to come.

7) Registration

These days, you need to provide at least two means of payment for an event: by check, or online.

By check is self-explanatory: provide an address and the payee to whom to write the check, and you're done.

For an online payment service, I prefer *Brown Paper Tickets* (brownpapertickets.com). Their fees are reasonable, attendees can pay either by credit card or into a PayPal account, and you can set up automatic thank-you messages with details about your event. It is a simple, self-explanatory system that allows you to set various ticket prices (as, for example, an "Early Bird" rate for early registrants, or a cut-rate price for children).

It is important to shut down registration about a week in advance of your event so you can pull together a master list of attendees, notify the food provider of how many attendees there will be, etc.

On the day of your event when your attendees arrive, perform check-in for them at a registration table set up at the entrance to the venue. This is the place where they sign up for a community service shift (if you're expecting that), get oriented to the site, are given some kind of marker that shows they belong at your event (colored yarn tied around the wrist works fine), and fill out a liability waiver. *(You can find a standard event liability form for the State of California at the end of this document—if this is not pertinent to you, do an Internet search to find an appropriate event liability waiver for your jurisdiction.*

<u>Community service shifts</u> not only provide you with more labor to do the work of the event, they are a powerful way to build a sense of ownership of the event on the part of participants; a feeling that "we are all doing this together." Tasks can include meal preparation or clean-up, help with parking or registration, site clean-up at the end of the event, collecting the recycling and garbage for transport, or any other easy tasks that need to be done.

<u>8) Policies</u>

Every event needs policies in place to protect the organizers from liability and to ensure that participants understand their responsibilities. Here are some examples of policies you should develop; these should be included *in writing* in the printed event program. **Do not skip this step.** If problems arise, you will be both protected and empowered by having published policies in place:

Refunds; provide the date (typically, about a week before the event) up to which you will provide a full or partial refund to ticket purchasers who are unable to attend. This information should be provided in your registration system (See "Registration", above)

Policies relating to children: Parents are expected to keep track of their children and are responsible for their safety. Children under the age of 12 must be accompanied by an adult at all times.

Photography policies: Photography of attendees is permissible only with the prior approval of the subject of the photograph. Some of us are not "out" as Atheopagans in our daily lives and do not wish to become so through accidental display of a photograph taken at EVENT.

Conduct standards: It is the intent of the producers that EVENT will be a safe, responsible and egalitarian event. Accordingly, we have established the following code of conduct. At no time shall anyone attending EVENT engage in any of the following behaviors:

Physical or verbal threats of any kind

Harassment, bullying or coercion of any person in any way

Racial, religious, gender-based, sexual preference-based or ethnic slurs

Possession of firearms, knives or any other instrument used as a weapon

Defacing, damaging or destroying property

Fighting, annoying others through noisy or boisterous activities, or in any other way creating a disturbance which is disruptive or dangerous to others or the programmatic activities of EVENT.

Harassment includes, but is not limited to:

Verbal comments that reinforce social structures of domination [related to gender, gender identity and expression, sexual orientation, disability, physical appearance, body size, race, age, religion, [YOUR SPECIFIC CONCERN HERE].

Deliberate intimidation, stalking, or following

Harassing photography or recording

Sustained disruption of talks or other events

Inappropriate physical contact

Unwelcome sexual attention

Advocating for, or encouraging, any of the above behaviour

Participants asked to stop any harassing behavior are expected to comply immediately.

If a participant engages in harassing behavior, event organizers retain the right to take any actions to keep the event a welcoming environment for all participants. This includes warning the offender or expulsion from EVENT[with no refund].

Event organizers may take action to redress anything designed to, or with the clear impact of, disrupting EVENT or making the environment hostile for any participants.

We expect participants to follow these rules at all event venues and event-related social activities. We think people should follow these rules outside event activities too!

Reporting

If someone makes you or anyone else feel unsafe or unwelcome, please report it as soon as possible to EVENT staff. Harassment and other code of conduct violations reduce the value of our event for everyone. We want you to be happy at our event. People like you make our event a better place.

When taking a report, EVENT organizers will ensure you are safe and cannot be overheard. They may involve other organizers to ensure your report is managed properly. Once safe, we'll ask you to tell us about what happened. This can be upsetting, but we'll handle it as respectfully as possible, and you can bring someone to support you. You won't be asked to confront anyone and we won't tell anyone who you are.

Our team will be happy to help you contact hotel/venue security, local law enforcement, local support services, provide escorts, or otherwise assist you to feel safe for the duration of the event. We value your attendance.

9) Marketing

Marketing is promotion of your event so it will be well-attended.

Atheopagans are a pretty narrow market niche, so most of your marketing will be online. Use your social media accounts to promote your event to your like-minded friends. You can also post about your event to the Atheopaganism Facebook group (or the Atheopagans UK group), and submit a guest post about it to the Atheopaganism blog. There are multiple Pagan groups on Facebook—post to them, too.

You can also print flyers for posting or distribution at your local occult bookstore or esoteric store. See if the owner would like to present!

Marketing is a numbers game; you have to *keep promoting* in order for your message to get out. Encourage your friends to share to their friends.

Messaging matters! "Come celebrate Nature around the fire! Enjoy a weekend in the woods creating, singing, dancing and drumming! Meet new friends and learn about real-world, science-based ways of celebrating life!"

10) Other Considerations

Medical support. Things happen. People fall, they twist their ankles, they get poison oak or ivy, and sometimes worse. If possible—and certainly if you have a larger gathering of 100 people or more—it is advisable to have a nurse or doctor onsite. Be sure that you also have a plan thought out in advance for evacuating someone who needs to go to the hospital.

Weather. Nature is magnificent, but it just *doesn't care!* Sometimes the weather simply won't cooperate with plans, whether that means 100 degree temperatures or pouring rain or snow. Be prepared; to as great a degree possible, be able to restructure your event to adapt to the changed conditions. If truly dangerous conditions are forecast, be willing to cancel and reschedule your event: it's not worth taking risks with people's lives.

Insurance. I *strongly recommend* that you take out a liability insurance policy for your event. They're cheap—typically, $100 or less for a weekend—and they will give you peace of mind about those longshot possibilities that someone gets hurt. Do not assume that having attendees sign a liability waiver alone will protect you from liability; it won't.

RELEASE OF LIABILITY, PROMISE NOT TO SUE, ASSUMPTION OF RISK AND AGREEMENT TO PAY CLAIMS

Event: [TYPE NAME OF YOUR EVENT HERE]

In consideration for being allowed to participate in this Event, on behalf of myself and my next of kin, heirs and representatives, I release from all liability and promise not to sue the organizers of this Event, their employees, officers, directors, volunteers and agents (collectively "Organizers") from any and all claims, including claims of the Organizers' negligence, resulting in any physical or psychological injury (including paralysis and death), illness, damages, or economic or emotional loss I may s uffer because of my participation in this Event, including travel to, from and during the Event. I am voluntarily participating in this Event. I am aware of the risks associated with traveling to/from and participating in this Event, which include but are not limited to physical or psychological injury, pain, suffering, illness, disfigurement, temporary or permanent disability (including paralysis), economic or emotional loss, and/or death. I understand that these injuries or outcomes may arise from my own or other's actions, inaction, or negligence; conditions related to travel; or the condition of the Event location(s).

Nonetheless, I assume all related risks, both known or unknown to me, of my participation in this Event, including travel to, from and during the Event. I agree to hold the Organizers harmless from any and all claims, including attorney's fees or damage to my personal property, that may occur as a result of my participation in this Event, including travel to, from and during the Event. If the Organizers incurs any of these types of expenses, I agree to reimburse the Organizers. If I need medical treatment, I agree to be financially responsible for any costs incurred as a result of such treatment. I am aware and understand that I should carry my own health insurance. I am 18 years or older. I understand the legal consequences of signing this document, including (a) releasing the Organizers from all liability, (b) promising not to sue the Organizers, (c) and assuming all risks of participating in this Event, including travel to, from and during the Event. I understand that this document is written to be as broad and inclusive as legally permitted by the State of California. I agree that if any portion is held invalid or unenforceable, I will continue to be bound by the remaining terms. I have read this document, and I am signing it freely. No other representations concerning the legal effect of this document have been made to me.

Participant Signature:

_____

Participant Name (print):_____

Date: _____

Ritual Music Recommendations

The music below was recommended by members of the Atheopagan Facebook group for use in Atheopagan rituals. Particularly in solitary rituals (when, obviously, having live accompaniment isn't possible), the addition of a musical "soundtrack" can be tremendously powerful. Also listed are some sources for chants which can be used in group rituals—singing is one of the most powerful ways to bring people together and build the sense of energy in a ritual!.

Adiemus (Karl Jenkins): *The Journey*

Anonymous4: Many disks of this a cappella women's medieval music ensemble could work well for ritual; I prefer *11,000 Virgins: Chants for the Feast of St. Ursula* by Hildegard von Bingen

Bare Necessities: *Take a Dance*. This ensemble plays traditional tunes for English country dancing. This album is lovely for High Spring or May Day celebrations; very light and springy.

Bone Poets Orchestra: *Atheist Anthems*

Chandra, Sheila: *A Bonecronedrone* and *The Zen Kiss*. Very trance-y.

Cossu, Scott with Eugene Friesen: *Reunion*. Light, quiet-morning piano with cello, good for reflection and introspective work.

Coyle, T. Thorn and Knight, Sharon: *Songs for the Strengthening Sun* and *Songs for the Waning Year* (both available at Bandcamp)

Dead Can Dance: many, many tracks; the two albums best suited are *The Serpent's Egg and In the Realm of a Dying Sun*

Darwin Song Project: *"You May Stand Mute" "Mother of Mystery"* and *"Clock of the World"*.

Delerium: *Karma.* Dance-y, trance-y. The track "Euphoria (Ecstacy)" is particularly good.

Daemonia Nymphe: Plays authentic instruments and sing hymns from ancient Greece.

Gabriel, Peter: *Passion* (soundtrack to "The Last Temptation of Christ")–hands down my favorite for solitary ritual.

Figueras, Montserrat and La Capella Reial de Catalunya: *El Cant de la Sybil-la.* 15th and 16th century "Songs of the Sybil". Powerful ritual music.

Libana: *Fire Within.* Not all tracks, but several are great for ritual.

Mayer, Peter: Naturalistic hymns, *"Blue Boat Home"*, *"Holy Now"* and *"Church of the Earth"* (and "God is a River" for Pantheists)

McBride, Abbi Spinner: *Fire of Creation and Family of Fire.* These are great chants, many of them without reference to divinity or "spirit".

McCutcheon, John: *Step by Step*

Pook, Joselyn: *Masked Ball* (from the soundtrack to "Eyes Wide Shut")

Portishead: *Dummy.* Dark, dreamy.

Reclaiming Collective: Some (not all) of the chants on *Let It Begin Now: Music from the Spiral Dance* (there are alternative Atheopagan lyrics to "This Ae Neet" in the Atheopagan Hymnal)

Roach, Steve: *On This Planet, Minimal*

Roach, Steve and Vir Unis: *Blood Machine*

Roth, Gabrielle and the Mirrors: all of her disks, which are themed on different ritual "flavors"

Sacred Treasures: *Choral Masterworks from Russia.* Russian Orthodox choral works by Rachmaninoff, Tchaikovsky and others. Magnificent.

Shibaten: haunting Digeridoo music.

Sovosó: Track "Dirt" on album *Then and Now.*

Vas: *Sunyata* and *Offerings* (highly meditative).

Winston, George: *The Seasons Cycle.* These four albums— *Autumn, December, Winter* into *Spring,* and Summer—are all lovely accompaniments for ritual work.

An Atheopagan Hymnal

Songs, Poems and Liturgy for Ritual Use by
Earth-Honoring Atheists

by Mark Green

Cosmos, I am a whirl of conceits
Saying "I" when I
Am only a moment of You.

General and Non-Seasonal

An Arrival/Presence Affirmation

We are sentient beings of Planet Earth, present in this place, this moment. The Cosmos is above us, the Earth is below us, and Life is around us. Here the wise mind unfolds. Here the playful child creates. Here the wondering human gazes out to view the vast and mighty Universe. We are here, and together.

An Arrival/Presence Meditation

Breathe this air. Remember that as you breathe, this grass and you, the trees yonder and you are blurring one into another, becoming something larger than either of you alone. You are giving each other life, one to the other.

Feel the sun on your head and your back. Feel the heat that beats against the insides of your clothes, the insides of your shoes. Remember that you are a controlled burn of food made of sunlight, that you and the sun are burning to live, to give the light that you make for the tiny time you can.

Remember the water you drink, the shower you took this morning. More than 80% of you is rain. Which is river. Which is ocean.

Feel the ground now, pressing on the soles of your feet, gravity pulling you close, each of us drawn down to stand the way iron filings stand on a magnet. Know that below us, the layer we call topsoil is made of the fertile bones of all that has come before us, the tiny and the mighty, and that they are all feeding us now.

Remember where you are. *[Insert qualities and landscape features of area where ritual is being held]* Remember how good it is to be in this place.

Open your eyes. Look around, and remember that you are alive. Many of you know one another, and many do not. All the moments of your life have brought you to here, to this instant. Be joyous in this moment. Welcome.

An Atheopagan Pledge of Allegiance

I pledge my service to Life on Earth

And the greater joy of Humanity

And for the Cosmos of which we are part

Awe, wonder, honor and reverence

So long as I am gifted this life.

A Benediction/Ritual Closing

To enrich and honor the gift of our lives, to chart a kind and true way forward, by these words and deeds we name intent: to dare, to question, to love. *(Unison all celebrants)*: May all that must be done, be done in joy. We go forth to live!

An Atheopagan Meal Blessing

This food, swelling from the Earth by the breath of the Sun, is brought to us by many hands. May all be honored. *(unison:)* We are grateful to eat today.

My Planet is a Rock

(Tune: My God is a Rock—traditional spiritual)

My planet is a rock, and it whirls in space,
It whirls in space, oh it whirls in space.
My Planet is a rock, with a sweet green face
The miracle where I was born.

My Sun it is a star, burning in the sky,
Burning in the sky, oh burning 'way up high.
My Sun it is a star, burning in the sky,
The nourisher of all we know.

Translation (poem)

It sounds cold

But when I see trees moving in wind, or

The spreading rings of waves across a pond I think

Math. And my heart swells with it:

Drawing curves limned by constraints, by limits and
boundaries,

Describing topographies as they

—fractals themselves—

Arc and swoop, dance the happy energized air about them.

All the words we have feel small and steel:

Plotting. Geometry.

Why not say instead,

The language of Creation sings in numbers:

The Voice of Being deeming

IT IS in song ephemeral and exquisite

Graphing its beauty across the sunset sky.

This is the Place (Song; still needs a tune)

This is the place

This is the place, oh yes

This is the place my life has led me to.

This is the time

This is the time, oh yes

This is the time to do what we must do.

This is the moment

This is the moment, oh yes

This is the moment, right here, right now.

The Journey (Song; still needs a tune)

We are Cro-Magnons who flew to the Moon

We are the Parents of those yet unborn

We are the Makers of wonders unseen

We are the Delvers into the unknown.

Here in this world fraught with wonder and terror

We are a species of beauty and horror

We choose a way, that we may all be better

Our path is grateful, and humble, with honor.

We are the women courageous and strong

We are the men who know beauty and tears

We are the love that binds families together

We carry love for the World, all our years.

It is so beautiful. It is so beautiful.

It is so beautiful. Hard though it is.

It is so generous; it is so generous

 it is so generous; living on Earth.

Blessed—a Benediction

I am among the blessed.

I am of the kind who leaves the glaring tube, remembering

And goes to watch the moon rise silver through the trees

Breathing purple and chill, stinging pine. I am

Among the blessed: I know the acacia, the first daffodil,

The irises unsheathing cream and violet labia in the green wet of May.

I tune for the new music on the radio: I turn it up.

I am among the blessed: I drink wine by firelight, clothes rank with smoke,

Bright silver twisted through my lobes. I know secrets;

They are tattooed on my body where the sleeves can cover them,

They read

Blessed, and only if we are lucky enough, you and I, courageous enough

To shed our clothes together will you read them. Seeing scarlet leaves drift down,

Perhaps, with ice around the moon, or the steel bones of the oaks against Orion,

Knowing we are among the blessed, that we miss nothing, that we will eat this life

Like a chocolate mango, like Beethoven ice cream,

Moaning our joy with each sweet bite.

Curiosity and Courage (Tune: Battle Hymn of the Republic)

Galileo had a telescope he pointed to the sky

And he saw the planets moving in a way that did deny

That the Earth was at the center of all that we can espy

And Science goes marching on!

Chorus:

Curiosity and Courage! Curiosity and Courage!

Curiosity and Courage!

And Science goes marching on!

Isaac Newton had conviction that all Nature works by laws

He worked out the mathematics, and made calculus because

Any theory made without it would be riddled through with flaws

And Science went marching on!

Charles Darwin understood that by selection life evolved

And the theory on which biology was based was solved

Once again, it's not humanity 'round which the world revolves

This Science goes marching on!

Marie Curie was a chemist with an active fascination

For the heavy kinds of isotopes that give off radiation
Nuclear science has since delivered us both awe and conflagration
Its Science goes marching on!

Albert Einstein saw the Cosmos in space/time dimensions four
And he proposed Relativity and opened up the door
To the Quantum world we'd never had a clue about before
Whose Science goes marching on!

As the theories of our Universe are sharpened year by year
We are learning mighty truths that scientists would have us hear
It's a simply wondrous Cosmos and magnificent Earth here
As Science goes marching on!

Boiling Up (The Complexity Song)

Chorus:

Boiling up, boiling up, boiling up from what came before

The Universe is making something new

Boiling up, boiling up, complex structures from simple forms

Galaxies and stars and planets, me and you.

It's funny when you think about it, but simple things tend to combine

Assemble in surprising ways and new

Two clear gases make up water; billions of cells you and I

Since the Big Bang that's what matter has to do.

Particles combine in gases, burn in stars to metal ash

Metals form in planets as years pass
Stars collecting into galaxies which superclusters form
At every scale these nesting structures make our home.

Tiny microorganisms join in colonies to grow
Specializing then they grow as one
Over millions years' evolving, diverse life is what we know
We're descended from those humble cells begun.

Down to the River to Sing

(Tune: Down to the River to Pray)

I went down to the river to sing
Feeling as one with everything
And what should I see but a red-tailed hawk
Oh Earth, beauty today

O sisters let's go down,
Let's go down, come on down,
O sisters let's go down,
Down to the river to sing

As I went down to the river to sing
Feeling as one with everything
And what should I see but a great osprey
O Earth, beauty today

Oh, brothers let's go down,
Let's go down, come on down,
O brothers let's go down,
Down to the river to sing.

As I went down to the river to sing

Feeling as one with everything

And what should I see but a leaping fish

O Earth, beauty today

O fathers let's go down

Let's go down, come on down,

O fathers let's go down

Down to the river to sing.

Yes I was down at the river to sing

Feeling as one with everything

And what should I see but a shooting star

O Earth, beauty today

O mothers let's go down,

Let's go down, come on down

O mothers let's go down

Down to the river to sing.

I was down at the river to sing

Knowing I'm a part of everything

And what should I see but the setting sun
O Earth, beauty today.

O children let's go down,
Let's go down, come on down,
O children let's go down,
Down to the river to sing.

Gimme a Godless Religion

Gimme a godless religion

Gimme a godless religion

Gimme a godless religion

That's good enough for me.

It's good enough for a skeptic

Whose reason is antiseptic

But whose needs are still eclectic

So that's good enough for me.

It was good enough for Sagan

Who was certainly no Pagan

He made science a contagion

And that's good enough for me.

It's not good enough for Dawkins

With his babe-bathwater squawkin'

How I wish he would stop talkin'!

That'd be good enough for me.

For progressives it is favored

For it has no biased flavor
Yes, equality we savor
And that's good enough for me.

We do rituals 'round the Focus
It's a symbol-laden locus
So dispense with hocus-pocus
It's good enough for me.

In our rituals we seek Presence
And a sense of pure transcendence
For the Earth is filled with pleasance—
That's good enough for me.

The Black Box

We're glowing, the Focus is glowing, we're knowing
Connection with all and with everything growing
All Presence, no thinking, we move to the beat
Alive, filled with wonder, a deep truth and sweet
So what is it? This thing that makes ritual power
And honeyed love flower, that slows down the hour,

It's not esoteric, it's not hard to find;
The black box isn't magic: it's your mind.

We're dancing, the fire is dancing, we're chanting
We're stamping and prancing and chanting and trancing
All Presence, no thinking, moving to the drum
And each of us family, each of us come
To this life unique. What is it? That so
Makes our pulses beat, helps us to grow

It's not esoteric, it's not hard to find
The black box isn't magic: it's your mind.

We're singing, our bodies are singing, the ringing

Of bells and the booming of drums is the pinging
Of Life in our bodies, of joy in our living
Of gratitude for all the Cosmos is giving
What is it? The secret ingredient here
That fills us with Presence and strips away fear?

It's not esoteric. It's not hard to find
The black box isn't magic: it's your mind.

It's real, it's all so incredibly Real, this moment
Of sharing and dancing and focus and foment
And humans have known it, since thousands of years
We do this: we're human, our laughter and tears
Cry, what is it? What makes this so moving and real
That fills us with such deep permission to feel?

It's not hocus pocus or gods, you will find:
The black box isn't magic: it's your mind.

Traditional and popular songs for rituals

Good ritual music usually shares some commonalities: it is easy for a group to learn, emotional in tone and usually with a compelling, driving rhythm. There are exceptions, of course: polyphonic chant is great ritual music, and has none of these characteristics.

Here are some traditional and popular songs which will work well in Atheopagan rituals:

Almost Home (Mary Chapin Carpenter)

An Unfinished Life (Kate Wolf)

Blue Boat Home (Peter Mayer)

The Chemical Elements (Tom Lehrer)

The Galaxy Song (Monty Python)

Imagine (John Lennon)

Keep Your Lamp Trimmed and Burning (trad. spiritual)

The Red-Tailed Hawk (Kate Wolf)

Science is Real (They Might Be Giants)

This Little Light of Mine (trad. spiritual)

This May Be the Last Time (trad. spiritual)

What a Wonderful World (Louis Armstrong)

Yule

Traditional/Popular songs usable for Atheopagan rituals: wintry non-religious songs such as Sleigh Ride.

Axial Tilt (Tune: Silent Night)

Axial tilt

The way the world's built:

Sun is north, then sun is south.

Axial precession makes seasons occur;

Sometimes bikinis and other times fur.

Insert metaphor here!

Insert metaphor here.

Evergreen tree

Holly berry

Stuff that stays alive, you see.

Meanwhile freezing and darkness reign

We'd much rather have fun than complain.

We are still alive!

We are still alive.

We're so hoping

Soon will come Spring

Meanwhile let's eat, drink, and sing!

Friends and family convene by the fire
Cold and darkness don't seem quite so dire.
Pass the gravy please!
Pass the gravy please.
(repeat first verse)

Oh Darkest Night (tune: O Holy Night)
Oh darkest night, the stars are brightly shining
It is the night of the dawning new year.
Here in the dark, for sun and warmth we're pining
But we are cheered by our friends and family here.
The cold bright stars: a trillion worlds above us
As here on Earth we gather loved ones near.
Raise up your eyes, and see the Cosmos' wonder
Oh Night sublime
Oh night, oh darkest night
Oh Night sublime
Oh night, oh night sublime.

Tonight We Sing (tune: Deck the Halls)

Tonight we sing, the old year passes! Fa la la la la, la la la la!

Celebrate ye lads and lasses! Fa la la la la, la la la la!

Wonder, family and presents! Fa la la la la, la la la la!

Wassailing like olden peasants! Fa la la la la, la la la la!

Celebrate critical thinking! Fa la la la la, la la la la!

Stuff your face, then do some drinking! Fa la la la la, la la la la!

Gather ye Atheopagans! Fa la la, la la la, la la la!

Starry night and brimming flagons! Fa la la la la, la la la la!

See the raging Yule log 'fore us! Fa la la la la, la la la la!

Hack the lyrics, join the chorus! Fa la la la la, la la la la!

Awe and merriment in measure! Fa la la la la, la la la la!

Gather close in Yuletide pleasure! Fa la la la la, la la la la!

(repeat first verse)

O Little Creatures of the Earth by Nels Olson
(Tune: O Little Child of Bethlehem)

O, little creatures of the Earth,
How wondrous are our lives!
From dust of stars far beyond Mars
Somehow were cast our dies.
Now in our precious time here,
Our consciousness brings light
To all that happens, near and far,
With meanings we define.

With care for what sustains our lives,
We watch our world in awe
And gratitude for all the warmth
That pours down from our star.
Its periodic movements
From our perspective here
Give cause for celebrations
Each season of the year!

O, shining star in solstice time,

Your radiant hours are few.
You turn and strike the New Year's chime
We owe our lives to you.
These darkest days of winter,
We miss your warming rays.
But every year this hemisphere
Returns to brighter days.

Since olden days the human race
Has feared your warmth would die.
The evergreen is ever seen
As hope we will survive.
With ancient drums still beating,
But superstitions dropped,
We send our heartfelt blessings
For peace, goodwill to all.

Mulled Wine (poem)

It begins where the smoke hits your eyes: smouldering
peat,

Mutton stew on a broad iron hook,

Deep snow. How can it ever have been summer?

Apples wrinkling and mice in the barley—

With so much to fear, thank the gods for company!

We'll tell our tales, remember how we passed the cold

Last year, and the year before.

And those who couldn't.

The grape leans across

The seasons, clasps the hand of summer's

Dried rind, dreaming the new fruit,

Calling the sun back,

World without end amen.

Riverain

Traditional/Popular songs usable for Atheopagan rituals for this season: Singin' In the Rain; Old Man River; Here Comes the Rain Again; It's Raining, It's Pouring; Have You Ever Seen the Rain

Invocation for Riverain

O Fog

Dragging your cloak, setting sudden claws, come

And wrap a winter's mystery 'round this house.

Rise soft in hollows. Open hushed roads.

Make the world a soft and pliant place

Fertile for dreams. Fertile.

Rain, thundering oak

Pounding the roof as you walk,

Come pour your seed, green Earth's round body

With all that will and can be.

Please us with streams' laughing

And the hope of something new.

O Fog, O Rain, in your green ardor

Come

(I am calling you, I am calling you)

Come kiss my face.

Vigil (poem)

Winter stands in the corner of my garden,

Rounds her shoulders, tucks her chin, draws tight her
cloak of stars and ice,

Razor moon and rain. Spare and erect, gaunt in the darkness,

Bark-peeling with moss predation, slick and black she
nods,

She waits, she leans,

The sky shows her jewelry, vents its wet moods. Death
litters

The paths with bones and brown rags. Secret life skulks
then like a thief:

She finds mushrooms between her toes, grows green and
furry slippers.

Long, long.

Until one day the clearwashed air grows sweet and yellow

With acacia, and her memory stirs with the taste

Of a near-forgotten lover's scent, feels again the warmth of
his regard,

And she stretches,

Stretches to find him again,

Turning up her daffodil face.

A Riverain Blessing (poem)

Three percent is all they say

The sweet water of a water planet

Three percent

The cool drink, the soft rain

Rare as blood, rare as luck, rare

To our wet hands, shining.

From the far sky, adrift in curds and blankets

Whips and knots, anvils towering thunder hammers

Rain the hand of kindness down

To our fields, our mouths, the dancing springs

And cold rivers, snaking the glens of Earth to the sky
again.

Do we take you for granted, O three percent?

Do we curse you for flooding, pop our grumbrellas

On a wet walk to the office?

Not I.

Not when puddles leap for joy and silver makes the sky

A treasury. I tip my face to you, and appearances be
damned

This gift is too precious: oceans' breath, sky's milk

Rivers' song falling drop by drop
To my waiting skin.

High Spring

Traditional/Popular songs usable for Atheopagan rituals for this season: April Showers; Here Comes the Sun;

A Spring Chant

It's coming! It's coming!

The light is returning

The leaves and the flowers

The oaks and green bowers

With bright purple crocus

To lay on the Focus

And warm days and bright

To bring us delight.

It's coming! It's coming!

The year is returning

The birds will be nesting

And we will be festing!

Go cold! Go dark!

The growing year's bright spark

Says Hello, Hello, Hello!

And round we go

Round we go

Round we go to the summer!

Another Spring Chant

These seeds, these eggs

Sprouting roots and limbs and legs

These days, these rites

Bringing forth a future bright

These hands, these hearts

Hopes and plans and works and arts

These hearts, these minds

Loving sharing humankind

These notes, this tune

March and April, May and June

This Earth, these stars

What a wonder, world of ours!

Spring Laughter (poem)

It begins with a giggle:

The tiniest white tendril reaching from the secret soil

Like a child's laugh, the purr of a cat and then

Raising, greening leaves peal across the meadows,

Carpet even what was once severe, sere,

Frowning brown in summer's dry thatch,

A deep belly rumble of soaring chlorophyll

Spreading wanton leaves, dangling perfumed sex

Climbing to nod and wave come and get me,

These meadows,

Brazen to the skip of children gathering posies

Bees lumbering slow in the crisp morning air

You, and I, perhaps, gone down to the stream

To lay down in that place, screened by waving rye

And the laughter of the stream gurgling out like a baby's delight

Playing with our playthings as we do, exploring

The whole world green and gripped with the howl of it:

Spring come at last.

May Day

Traditional/Popular songs usable for Atheopagan rituals for this season: : Hal an Tow; Abbott's Bromley Horn Dance; Sumer is Icumen In; I Can See Clearly Now; Let the Sunshine In;

May Morning (poem)

Fresh as the day the world was made,

This morning: dew-spattered through feather fans

Of foxtail and wild rye. Mars is low on the horizon, for once. Still

As a caught breath, the day, hushed,

Holds for a slow-golding time, the rose hints

Of bold and bright to come, of music

Yet to be made, dances old as the village, new as tomorrow's milk.

How can it be, four billion, five hundred million years, the old

and battered Earth,

Veteran of ice and fire, meteor, petroleum, stupidity, avarice, ignorance

How can it be, this innocence: ryetops waving hello, good morning,

224

Beads of crystal dew filled with beauty wash*,
The bright face of the Golden One coming,
Bringing suit to his blue lover again,

And Earth meeting him with an armload of flowers
As if all the grief were undone, as if
(As it is)
The sorrows and losses don't matter, really,
Not in the face of this coming morning

When Earth says Yes
Sun says I Am Here
The great rounding of things stately in its time,
The lone bird calling to a lightening sky

He is risen
He is risen

*It is an old European tradition that dew gathered on May Day morning will enhance beauty.

Midsummer

Traditional/Popular songs usable for Atheopagan rituals for this season: Summertime; Summer Breeze;

Midsummer Carol (Tune: Deck the Halls)

Mow the lawn and trim the yew hedge! ! Fa la la la la, la la la la!

Break, and have a frosty beverage! Fa la la la la, la la la la!

Mount the chaise lounge and the hammock! Fa la la la la, la la la la!

Toast the year with gin and tonic! Fa la la la la, la la la la!

Dive the cooling pool before us! Fa la la la la, la la la la!

Dance the sun down with the Morris! Fa la la la la, la la la la!

Sizzling food is on the Barbie! Fa la la la la, la la la la!

Maybe play a game of bocce! Fa la la la la, la la la la!

Hit the road for a vacation! Fa la la la la, la la la la!

Now's the time for recreation! Fa la la la la, la la la la!

Time for folly and adventure! Fa la la la la, la la la la!

'Fore we return to indenture! Fa la la la la, la la la la!

Summer's End

Traditional/Popular songs usable for Atheopagan rituals for this season: John Barleycorn Must Die; Hammer and a Nail (Indigo Girls);

Harvest

Traditional/Popular songs usable for Atheopagan rituals for this season:: Miri It Is; John Barleycorn Must Die;

The Apple Tree Wassail (English Traditional)

O lily-white lily, o lily-white pin,

Please to come down and let us come in!

Lily-white lily, o lily-white smock,

Please to come down and pull back the lock!

Chorus:

(It's) Our wassail jolly wassail!

Joy come to our jolly wassail!

How well they may bloom, how well they may bear

So we may have apples and cider next year.

O master and mistress, o are you within?

Please to come down and pull back the pin

Chorus

There was an old farmer and he had an old cow,

But how to milk her he didn't know how.

He put his old cow down in his old barn.

And a little more liquor won't do us no harm.

Harm me boys harm, harm me boys harm,

A little more liquor won't do us no harm.

Chorus

O the ringles and the jingles and the tenor of the song goes

Merrily merrily merrily.

O the tenor of the song goes merrily.

Spoken:

Hatfulls, capfulls, three-bushel bagfuls,

Little heaps under the stairs.

Hip hip hooray!

Hallows

Traditional/Popular songs usable for Atheopagan rituals for this season: Angel of Bells;

This Ae Neet (Tune: the Lyke-Wake Dirge: Yorkshire traditional)

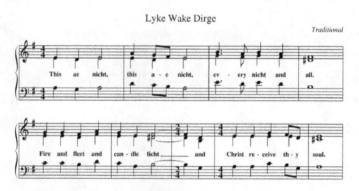

Lyke Wake Dirge

Traditional

This ae nicht, this a - e nicht, ev - ery nicht and all.

Fire and fleet and can - dle licht____ and Christ re - ceive th - y soul.

This version based on the first verse as sung by The Young Tradition
The lyrics are adapted from Aubrey's manuscript version of 1686.
The tune was noted by Hans Fried, who heard it from an old Scots lady, Peggy Richards.

THIS ae neet, this ae neet,

Every neet and alle,

Fire and sleet and candle-leet,

And Earth receive thy bones.

O thou whose time on Earth has passed

Every neet and all

With silent supper we break your fast*

May Earth receive thy bones.

230

Thy cold clay limbs with shroud we entwine
Every neet and all
And thy bright face will live in our minds
Though Earth receive thy bones.
If e'er thou had ought cause to despair
Every neet and all
All debts and sorrows now have repair
May Earth receive thy bones.

Though this neet thou art not alive
Every neet and all
By tales and memories shalt thou survive
May Earth receive thy bones
        (continues next page)
This ae neet, this ae nicht,
Every neet and alle,
Fire and sleet and candle-leet,
And Earth receive thy bones.

Notes: ae: one; neet: night; sleet: salt; leet: light. * Refers
to the Pagan Hallows tradition of the silent or "Dumb
Supper", wherein a place is set for the dead.

Mystery—a poem cycle

(For Pat and Jeff Winters, in memory of their son Braggi)

I. Wail

Encompass this: as an egg snake
Swallowing a jagged, broken stone would unhinge,
Unhinge and stretch
But cannot swallow without blood and scar.
Stretch your mouth until the howl is your dark heart's
blood
Poured on the floor of the world.
Tear the words from the walls of your body:
Never. Never. Forever.

II. Dark Road

Without notice, he turned from us,
Not a backward glance, and lit a lantern to walk
Into that dark country. We could see his light awhile.
It grew far and faint, then gone. We followed seven steps,
As far as bloodwarmed feet could take us. Time changed.

Nothing mattered.
Dust became the clotting of everything, and the sweet

232

Temple scent of myrrh, lavender, lotus, the dimness
Of candleglow became a comfort:
Easier to stay, lay the long bones down,
Light a lantern, walk the dark road too.

III. Pulse

The world's insistence thrums in the body
And denies surrender: the mouth craves food,
The ear speech, the eye color. My loves,
Yet living,
Called me to set the long pendulum swinging again,
To retrace my steps from the dark:
One, another.
A month from now, perhaps two more.

The seventh, though, will never return.
One foot, informed,
Remains upon the track he left
When first he turned his face from us.

IV. Grace

In the stark room at her center—

The innermost coffin, alabaster still,
Without which howl the ten thousand bereftitudes—
In that most private chamber comes a grace
That is the knowing of what must be.

Here no wars are fought with what is.
Here there is only knowledge.

She finds her love there, opens her hands,
Knowing what must be done.

V. Hole

And so it is seen, gazing down to the bottom
Of that forever hole, that our world,
Seeming so substantial, is yet hollow, a crust
Thin and fragile and subject to sinkhole
Without notice or reason. The hollow world holds us,
A bubble of clay above the falling darkness whose mouth
We mark with stones and flowers.

In the bottom is a dark mirror. Dimly, through a smoke
Gaze of averted eyes and cobbled tales we speak

To ease the awful finality of it, comes a face: mine.

Yours. All of ours, all we love, in time:

And not much of it. To look down where the flowers,

Where the swathed limbs make the shape of living

And yet are not, will never live again

Is the seen truth, the known pattern of all precious and
guarded things.

VI. Kyrie

O dark and odious inscrutable Force

Whose disembodied Name we cannot know, but fear:

Hear me.

My pious acceptances are a tissue of flimsy thoughts.

I hate and fear You utterly.

I plead, though You give no thought to mercy,

For mercy.

I pray, though You show no sign of kindness,

For kindness.

Midnight Stair (tune: Going Home on the Morning Train)

I'm going down that midnight stair
I'm going down that midnight stair
I'm going down that midnight stair
When your time comes, you're going to join me there
All my pain's been taken away
Taken away.

You must carry on, must carry on
You must carry on, must carry on
You must carry on must carry on
You must live though I am gone
All my pain's been taken away
Taken away

I'm gone away, won't be back again
I'm gone away, won't be back again
I'm gone away, won't be back again
Remember me, remember when
All my pain's been taken away
Taken away.

Example Rituals

A Ritual for Joy

Arrival: As participants proceed toward the ritual ground where the ritual will take place, each is met by a pair of participants who smoke-bless and asperge them.

After being smoke-blessed and asperged, participants stand in a circle around the Focus or a laid but unlit fire, holding hands and with their eyes closed.

The convener/coordinator of the ritual says: "We are sentient beings of Planet Earth, present in this place, this moment. The Cosmos is above us, the Earth is below us, and Life is around us. Here the wise mind unfolds. Here the playful child creates. Here the wondering human gazes out to view the vast and mighty Universe. We are here, and together."

The participants repeat, "We are here, and together," and open their eyes.

Qualities: Another participant (different from the convener/coordinator) says, "May we know and embody these Qualities, that our rites guide us forward to achieve our dreams and better the world."

Participants then call out Qualities they wish to include, such as reverence, courage, abundance, health, etc.

Intentions: Convener/coordinator states the purpose of the ritual: "Our intent today is to align ourselves with the spirit of joy: to bring joy into our lives and between us, and express our desire that the world know more joy."

Participants sing song, "This is a Song for Joy".

If possible, this is the point at which a fire may be lit in the center of the circle to express the igniting of Intention. If not, the Focus is constructed at the center of the circle and candles may be lit. A slow drumbeat begins as the song ends.

Deep Play: As soon as the Intention has been stated, drummer(s) strike up a lively beat (or recorded dance music is played, depending on what is available), and the participants release holding hands and begin to dance around the circle.

This portion of the ritual can go on for ten minutes or four hours, depending on time available and the wishes of the participants. If a longer ritual, quiet periods when people may speak or sing are interspersed between periods of drumming and/or dance. Participants are free to leave the circle to take a rest break, drink water or eat, etc., but should make an effort not to distract from what is going on in the circle while so engaged. To remain a part of the larger process, those who do not feel like dancing may stand at the edge of the circle and shake a rattle, or may join the drummers in drumming.

A signal is played to warn drummers and dancers to wind down a few minutes before the end of Deep Play: this can be a bell, a gong, a particular drum rhythm, etc.

The participants reform in a circle, holding hands.

Gratitude: Going around the circle, each participant states her/his name and something for which s/he is grateful.

Benediction: The convener/coordinator says, "To enrich and honor the gift of our lives, to chart a kind and true way forward, by these words and deeds we name intent (*participants join in unison*): to dare, to question, to love. May all that must be done, be done in joy. We go forth to *live!*"

The Jewel: A Solitary Ritual for Personal Growth and Healing

This is a solitary ritual especially recommended for those who struggle with suffering due to past abuse or neglect.

Arrange a Focus with a mirror in the center, flanked by candles, and a cup or chalice of wine or flavorful juice. Burn a delicious-smelling incense: I recommend Russian Orthodox incense (available at most Orthodox book stores) for this ritual. It may help to print the meditations on little cards and prop them against the bottom of the mirror so you can read them while maintaining your gaze on your reflection.

Close your eyes and concentrate on your breath–going in, and out, your clothes shifting as your chest rises and falls. Breathe deeply, from the belly. Feel where gravity holds you down against the Earth. Drink the good air and know it is a gift, a sustaining gift of the World to you. Wait until you are calm and centered, then open your eyes.

Gaze into your eyes in the mirror. Speak this meditation slowly and with measured cadence:

You are a jewel. Many facets, unique, an artwork of the Universe.

You are perfect. You are as you should be, in this moment.

You are loved. You are worthy of love.

You are a jewel. No other could replace you. You are welcome here.

Repeat seven times. You may feel tension and resistance as you say these words, because parts of you don't believe them. That's okay–the point of this ritual is to strengthen the parts that do.

After the seventh time, take and let out a deep breath. Then say,

I am a jewel. I am unique, an artwork of the Universe.

I am perfect. I am as I should be, in this moment.

I am loved. I am worthy of love.

I am a jewel. I belong here.

Repeat three times.

Close by sipping the wine or juice until it is gone. Know that this pleasure, this gift is your birthright: you deserve happiness.

Close your eyes and blow out the candles. The ritual is done.

The above examples are exactly that: examples. Cultures all over the world have created powerful, emotionally transformative rituals with wildly varying formats and practices, and one could spend a lifetime studying without getting to all of them. But this format will work—as a general structure, it is a map to a particular kind of territory. I invite and encourage you to experiment, bearing in mind the "ingredients" that make a ritual engaging and emotionally powerful.

The most important thing is to start. Religion is *practiced,* not just thought about or analyzed, and Atheopaganism is no different. Get your feet wet and your hands dirty, and try out some ritual techniques to see how they feel. Ritual arts require learning and practice like any other, so don't worry about it if some of the things you try don't work out as you'd expected or hoped.

Whatever your reservations, in nearly every case I guarantee you'll find the outcomes gratifying and illuminating.

Best of luck and experiences to you on the journey!

Online Resources

Atheopagan Facebook group: facebook.com/groups/atheopaganism

Atheopagan YouTube Channel: www.youtube.com/channel/UC0-weMipO8r3HUQzsaOQlSg

Atheopagan Goodreads page—nice long list of books pertinent to Atheopaganism: www.goodreads.com/group/show/158696-atheopaganism

Atheopagan Zazzle Store—Bumper stickers, pendants, buttons, mugs, Yule cards, t-shirts & more! www.zazzle.com/the_atheopagan_store

Humanistic Paganism blog: humanisticpaganism.com

Natural Pagan blog: naturalpagan.org

Natural Pagans Aggregation site: naturalpagans.com

Spiritual Naturalist Society: snsociety.org/

The Great Story–a naturalist cosmology: thegreatstory.org/what_is.html

Acknowledgements

In developing the thinking contained in this work, I am grateful to the authors of several books I found illuminating and thought-provoking, and which served as pointers to original scientific source material too extensive to list here.

Adler, Margot. *Drawing Down the Moon*. New York, NY: Beacon Press, 1979.

Dawkins, Richard. *The God Delusion*. Boston, MA: Mariner Books, 2008 (reprint edition).

Hutton, Ronald. *The Triumph of the Moon*. New York, NY: Oxford University Press, 1999.

Johnson, Steven. *The Ghost Map*. New York, NY: Penguin USA, 2004.

Marcus, Gary. *Kluge: The Haphazard Construction of the Human Mind*. New York, NY: Houghton Mifflin, 2008.

Sacks, Oliver. *The Man Who Mistook His Wife for a Hat, and Other Clinical Tales*. New York, NY: Touchstone, 1998.

Sagan, Carl. *The Dragons of Eden: Speculations on the Origins of Human Intelligence*. New York, NY: Random House, 1977.

Waldrop, M. Mitchell. *Complexity: The Emerging Science at the Edge of Order and Chaos*. New York, NY: Simon & Schuster, 1992.

Wolfram, Stephen. *A New Kind of Science*. Champaign,

IL: Stephen Wolfram LLC, 2002.

But more than anything, I am deeply grateful to those among my friends and in my community who helped me to arrive at the point of making this leap and articulating these thoughts (whether or not they agreed with them). Some had to put up with me as I went through the crisis that led to this investigation, and contributed to discussions which helped to inform my thinking as it developed.

Thanks to the pioneers of the modern nontheist Paganism movement: Aine Orga, John Halstead, Jon Cleland Host, Rua Lupa, Daniel Strain, Tom Swiss, Stephen Posch, Lupa Greenwolf and many others—I am sure to be forgetting some, so please forgive me.

Particularly, I thank the members of Dark Sun, the Fire Family community, Tonya Orin McNeese, Arwen Gwyneth, and most of all my wife and partner in crime, Nemea.

Thanks and much love to each of you.

Afterword

This is only the beginning, of course.

This book describes the bones of a path.

But the flesh of it is in the living.

There is a great deal more information about Atheopagan practices, rituals, philosophy and values at atheopaganism. org, and a community of more than 1,500 of us on Facebook.

We're all learning and practicing and evolving this way of living together, so join us! Be a part of the movement towards reality-based sacralizing of this holy Earth and life.

I look forward to encountering you if you choose to engage our growing community.

In any case…*go forth to live!*

Author Biographies

Mark A. Green is an activist, writer, poet, musician and lover of the Earth. Founding Executive Director of Sonoma County Conservation Action, he developed the organization into the largest environmental group on the North Coast of California, for which he was named the Sonoma County Environmentalist of the Year in 1997. He is the creator of the Atheopagan path and publishes at Atheopaganism.org, WitchesAndPagans.com, NaturalPagans.com and HumanisticPaganism.com, and serves as administrator of the online Atheopagan community on Facebook. He lives in the watershed of the Russian River with the delightful Nemea and Miri, the Very Soft Cat.

John Halstead is a native of the southern Laurentian bioregion and lives in Northwest Indiana, near Chicago. He is one of the founders of 350 Indiana-Calumet, which works to organize resistance to the fossil fuel industry in the Region. John was the principal facilitator of "A Pagan Community Statement on the Environment". He strives to live up to the challenge posed by the statement through his writing and activism. John is Editor-at-Large of HumanisticPaganism.com and edited the anthology, Godless Paganism: Voices of Non-Theistic Pagans.

Notes